STEEPED

STEEPED

ADVENTURES OF A TEA ENTREPRENEUR

BROOK EDDY

LIONCREST
PUBLISHING

STEEPED

Adventures of a Tea Entrepreneur

FIRST EDITION

Published by Lioncrest Publishing in the United States of America
Library of Congress Control Number: 2023913907

ISBN 978-1-5445-3871-6 *Hardcover*
      978-1-5445-4482-3 *Paperback*
      978-1-5445-3872-3 *Ebook*
      978-1-5445-4483-0 *Audiobook*

For Kathleen, Patricia, & Janet

CONTENTS

PROLOGUE...11

1. CHANT HARE KRISHNA AND BE HAPPY................... 13

2. CO-CONSPIRATORS 29

3. UNEXPECTED ENTREPRENEUR...............................39

4. WORK AS WORSHIP... 57

5. HOW I BUILT THIS...73

6. PUSHKAR 113

7. HIGHS & HEARTACHE..137

8. SABBATICAL 165

9. A ROLLING BOIL..175

EPILOGUE... 193

RECIPES 197

ACKNOWLEDGMENTS... 199

BIBLIOGRAPHY... 201

A woman is like a tea bag; you can't tell how strong she is until you put her in hot water.

—ELEANOR ROOSEVELT

PROLOGUE

My mother removed the screen from the second-floor bedroom window and jumped to the crunchy, frosted ground with me in her arms. Newspapers were starting to slap driveways, and honey-hued light appeared behind the lifeless, etched branches in the sky. My grandparents wouldn't find the cool, empty room for another three hours, and by then, we would already be in the front seat of a stranger's car with dry heat blasting our faces, heading west. My grandfather had just picked us up in Chicago a few days earlier after my mother called in a panic from a Greyhound bus station claiming men were after us.

It was 1974, and I was thirteen months old. My mother and I had spent the last six months traversing the country via truck drivers, strangers, hippie friends, and the Greyhound bus system. Some nights I was plopped down on a shag carpet surrounded by a haze of pot smoke while my mother strummed her dulcimer. Other nights, we camped on the beach in California with her boyfriend, the waves my lullaby, or we spooned in a trucker's sleeping cab as we rolled down the highway. Then, there were the afternoons in Denver and San Francisco where I was girdled to my mother's torso in Southwestern fabric, peering out as she distributed Kahlil Gibran's *The Prophet* to strangers on the street.

I will never know why she desperately clutched to that book's poetic reality while unhinged and dragging me around the country. What I do know is it took us four days of hitchhiking after escaping through the window of my grandparents' house to reach a small town in Colorado, and within a week, my mother was dead.

Those early seeds of travel would eventually set me on my path as an entrepreneur. While it was an early playbook stitched together with uncertainty, adventure, friends, love, abandonment, and grief, it was also a survival playbook. As a young person, I already knew inherently no problem was too big to solve, asking for help was a sign of strength, worry only shackled people with inaction, and one could always make a new life. Those hitchhiking days must have steeped fearlessness and adventure into me, and I was determined to take control of my life.

With no father listed on my birth certificate, I became a ward of the court and was adopted by my maternal grandparents. My bedroom became the same room my mother climbed out of that winter morning.

CHAPTER 1

CHANT HARE KRISHNA AND BE HAPPY

Bangalore, India, 2002

"It's hard to leave the comforts of the known. But on that ledge of the unknown—that's where life starts."

—JOSE ANDRES, CHEF AND WORLD CENTRAL KITCHEN FOUNDER

I was surprised when I walked out of the airport in Bangalore—not by the muggy air laced with the smell of burning trash and diesel, the nonstop honking, or the throngs of pushy men approaching me to get in their taxis—but to see a tall Caucasian man waving at me. He stood out—he was white and wiry and towered over everyone. Was that Sri Hari waving at me?

I was connected with him through a family friend, and he offered to show me around my first week in India before I headed north to work on a research project. From his name I had pictured an Indian man. He rushed toward me wearing apricot-colored flowy clothes, and his neck was heavy with beads. *Who was this dude?* I thought. He had a strong Eastern European accent and called me Brookie. *Russian*, I first thought. He smelled of incense and his green eyes were accentuated by his long, dark eyelashes. He was attractive and I suddenly felt self-conscious. I was sweating already from just standing outside. Not the dewy kind, but the dripping from my chin kind of sweat. I felt haggard from traveling and wasn't wearing my signature lipstick.

"Where are you from?" I immediately asked as soon as we settled into the tiny car. His knees almost touching the steering wheel.

"Croatia," he answered and smiled at me. Holding the stare a little too long.

"I wasn't expecting you would be Croatian... And how old are you?" I'm sure he could hear in my voice what I was really asking. *Are we similar in age and if yes, maybe we'll be lovers?*

"Twenty-eight," he answered.

"How fun, me too!"

We drove slowly through the crowded streets and it was like an explosion of color, smells, and sounds all around me. Wagons piled high with perfectly placed eggplants, onions, claws of ginger, and tomatoes. Flowers, like birthday streamers, dangled over storefronts and streets. Smoke poured out of stalls with the smell of fried food. Men everywhere, cows, mopeds, temples, yellow autorickshaws, goats, and bright flashes of color from women in saris dotting the streets. Honks punctuated our conversation. Nonstop beeps, pulsating little tweets, vibrating blurts of sound, quick honks like a forceful exclamation point at the end of a speech, and the occasional long, making-a-statement sort of honk.

We finally broke free and were on dusty dirt roads. Sri Hari used his windshield wipers to brush off the graham-cracker-like dust obscuring the windshield. Through wisps of flying hair, I saw acres of farms dotted with women workers. Soil speckled with saris, vibrant splatters of color on the lush canvas of India. I smelled brief patches of jasmine and then burning trash. I loved it all. I was on my adventure. I was untethered. I was traveling like I did that first year of my life, open and taking it all in. Although the transport was bumpy, and I had no idea where we were going, there were smiling faces surrounding me, exotic smells and newness everywhere—I felt free. And I was in control this time. Or so I thought.

We were staying in the home of an Indian family Sri Hari knew. I slept on a cushion on the floor that night, my backpack a pillow.

The next morning, I was awoken early to commence a daylong tour of temples. Couldn't I sleep for a few days? Have a leisurely breakfast at some café? On the inside I felt annoyed I couldn't do my usual independent swagger and was being told what to do. I wanted to know what temples and where and why? I felt like I was a hostage. But I was in India, and shouldn't act like a coddled, wimpy white girl. I decided I would "Let go and let India," and that became my first mantra of the trip.

Still blinking jet-lagged, dry eyes, I went into a dark room, and a woman named Kerela, the woman's floor I had slept on, wrapped me in one of her turquoise saris. Her mechanical hands hurried through, tucking and pleating fabric around my hips with half-opened eyes. She swiped crimson paint down the center of my forehead. It dried quickly and tightened my pores, pulling my third eye skin with a gentle tug. She tucked my blonde hair under a matching scarf and I could smell her fingers, wood fire and onion, and she said, "keep your hair tucked in like this."

Swaddled in my sari, I walked outside to the dark streets and saw a repurposed old short school bus, painted white and emblazoned with purple lettering: "Chant Hare Krishna and Be Happy." Inside were eight white Eastern European devotees, dressed in peach dhotis or long skirts. *What the hell*, I thought. *I may be a hostage after all. Isn't this actually a cult?* I was intrigued. Honestly, I loved cults. Ever since studying Jonestown at a Christian school in ninth grade as my research topic (my teacher did not appreciate my chosen topic and kept trying to offer other options), I had always wanted to go undercover in a cult. How did Jim Jones and David Koresh, and the Heaven's Gate convince so many people to follow them and die for them? Maybe this was my opportunity?

I had seen those bald hippies passing out free books in airports or sitting in chanting circles in documentaries about the seventies, that standard B role they use in all films mentioning Hare Krishnas. Or I'd seen them on Venice Beach years ago when I lived in California. But now they were up close. These were real Hare Krishnas.

While the sheen of the fabric felt wonderfully feminine, my legs were constricted to a dainty, small step and I had to waddle up the bus stairs. I thought, *No big strides today, no jumping over cow dung, no sprinting if the Hare Krishnas attempt to sell me.*

This was not how I had pictured my first day in India. I was unemployed, rudderless, and uncertain of my professional path forward after moving across the country for a development director job with an environmental radio show in Boulder, Colorado, only to be fired months later. I prided myself on being employment promiscuous, but *I* was usually the one to leave after a year or two for another opportunity. Not the other way around. It was humiliating. I was in the throes of my Saturn return (your astrological coming of age or a push toward adulthood), but I hadn't landed there yet. I had no money, no purpose, no home, and was straddled with $45,000 in student loan debt.

It wasn't until I heard a story on NPR—one of those classic driveway moments when I couldn't get out of the car until the story was over—that something shifted. I sat transfixed in my dented Subaru, learning about a group of people in India and a movement called Swadhyay (swad-ee-eye). They were transforming villages through collective farming and community fishing boats—all attempts to eliminate social disparity while cultivating community. They explained many of the world's problems could be eradicated by seeing each other as brothers and sisters, as a holy family, instead of the devices that separate us—like religion, caste, country, economics, sexual orientation, land, language, wokeness, politics, gender, culture, and color. It sounded like a salve the world needed and the inspiration I had been searching for.

This was one month after September 11, and the war in Afghanistan was ramping up. There was a massive anti-Muslim sentiment, and the chants for war and retribution were loud. While I didn't expect President Bush to roll the beads of his WWJD bracelet while considering alternatives to war, I had hoped more of the country would be antiwar.

Perhaps studying Swadhyay and going to India was the answer for me to find my purpose? It could be self-discovery dusted with volunteerism—everything I had hoped to get at grad school but didn't. Maybe this would make that student loan feel worth it. I felt a spark of inspiration and wanted to learn more.

Now, I was sitting in the back of a school bus in a form-fitting sari, learning how Sri Hari fell in love with Krishna and how that cured him of his existential crisis.

After a few hours in the school bus, we arrived at the temple. We removed our shoes before walking up the shiny glazed white stairs and entered a large, open-air temple. We sat and quickly joined another group, which consisted of four Indian men and ten young white men who couldn't have been over twenty-five. Being the only woman was starting to be a theme that would continue during my travels.

They all bowed and said, "Namaste."

That word wasn't just something to murmur at the end of a yoga class. When you say, "Namaste" to someone, you are saying that you see God in them. And when they say, "Namaste" to you, they are acknowledging and loving the God in you. It means "hello" in Hindi—even "hello" is meant to bring you back to the soul.

I learned that some of the young men were from Croatia, like Sri Hari, and others were from Serbia, Italy, the UK, and Slovenia. They each had a shiny shaved head with a tuft of hair at the back of the skull—a handle for God to grasp them and pluck them up to Nirvana. Shaving your head is not a rule, but many men living in the monastic or ashram environment do it. It signifies that they are devotees of Krishna[1] and distinguishes them from others who shave their heads completely such as Buddhists. Sri Hari had his tuft of hair spun around into a tiny man bun. A far more attractive choice, I thought. Krishna is a manifestation of the lord Brahma[2] and, according to the Bhagavad Gita, came to earth to show man the lessons for a sublime life through knowledge, compassion, humility, love, and devotion.

Soon, a few boys jumped up to grab instruments. It began with dainty dings from finger cymbals. Then the harmonium in

---

1 Dear reader, meet me down here from time to time for side notes or background information. Krishna, like Moses, was separated from his birth mother as a baby in a basket down a river in fear of a king declaring certain baby boys would be killed. He was raised in another community by foster parents and early in life was recognized as doing miracles, and his flute playing created ecstatic dancing. He taught Karma yoga (not the physical yoga we know as movement core power yoga, but a spiritual yoga of practicing nonattachment and removal of material gratification), Jnana yoga (self-realization through philosophical discussions), and Bhakti yoga (devotional service through prayer, dance, music, and kirtan). The word yoga in Sanskrit is to "yoke, unite, join." The union between the individual and the divine. Also, Krishna was a player! He had eight verified wives, and legend states thousands of junior wives. But the love of his life was Radha, who was married to another man.

2 Just as in Christianity, Hindu gods hold a trinity. Brahma is the creator not just of the universe, but of everything. Vishnu is the second member of the trinity and maintains order and harmony in the universe. Vishnu is worshipped in many forms and has several avatars or incarnations, but is far more elusive than the gods that preside over elements like earth, fire, rain, knowledge, compassion, and wealth. If Brahma is like the Judeo-Christian God, Vishnu is the Holy Spirit. Shiva rounds out the trinity as the destroyer. Shiva is not haphazard or malicious, but regenerative destruction. A death that is a rebirth. Sound familiar?

the center began to bleat. Drums slung around a few of the boys sitting in our circle joined with a sonorous sound, and then the shy tambourines waited patiently to crack into the song. Then the chanting erupted with the sixteen-word mantra: *"Hare Krishna, Hare Krishna, Krishna Krishna, Hare Hare, Hare Rama, Hare Rama, Rama Rama, Hare Hare."*

They swayed and rocked back and forth with bright eyes. An older man draped in saffron cloth chanted softly; his fingers caressed the tulsi wood Japa beads in the small bead bag looped around his neck, like the rounds of a rosary.

I joined in the chanting awkwardly. The first part was easy, but it took a few rounds to get the end part nailed. Once I was in rhythm with them, I felt a tickling hum in my lungs, a warm togetherness heating the back of my spine. All those *R*'s reverberating. The rounds went on and on for maybe twenty minutes. I closed my eyes and felt a beautiful comfort envelop me. It wasn't Krishna's sudden smile resting on my being, but a oneness transcending dogma—a timelessness when chanting. I did feel happy. Maybe there was something to this? Maybe this wasn't a cult, after all. Just as I felt reassured that I was in the groove of the chant, the harmonium slowed down and the chanting changed pace. One word stretched out—forever! Then, twenty minutes later, it sped back up again. My chanting got louder, my smile bigger, my heart lighter, and I understood why they did this. I caught Sri Hari looking at me. He definitely looked all blissed out, and I mouthed, "Thank you," with a beaming smile.

When the music became louder and the energy heightened, someone jumped up, and everyone began to dance. This *kirtan* was a type of devotion, offering, and communion. I was in the middle of South India, jumping up and down in a temple surrounded by Hare Krishnas. So random.

I watched these young men and wondered how they all got

here. What drove them to this ashram, to India, and to the Hare Krishna movement? Was there a magnetic pull they couldn't refuse? Was there some sort of Eastern European recruitment center? What made them give up college, jobs, alcohol, meat, girls, boys, drugs, and sex to come here and study, meditate, and chant? The answer was in the same founding principles of the Hare Krishna movement that first attracted Allen Ginsburg and George Harrison in the late sixties: transcendental chanting, meditation for inner peace—and the food.

TEMPLE FOOD: A MISSION

Once the dancing and chanting frenzy was over, we sat down, and some of the temple boys brought out buckets of food and began serving us breakfast: scoops of turmeric rice and curried potatoes and carrots on banana leaf plates or *patravali*. Sri Hari whispered in the back of my ear with his Croatian accent, "Ve eat with our hands. It makes food taste better." He then dropped two pieces of warm chapati bread on my banana leaf. I watched the boys in our circle dive in and scoop up the rice and potatoes with the chapati. I followed their lead and used the bread as a spoon, a vehicle for so many sublime flavors. The curry and ginger in the potatoes sparked brightness in my mouth. The warm bread felt like it was just baked, the edges still hot from the clay oven, and it was slathered with ghee. I watched them circle the rice on their plates with their fingertips, like twisting off a cap, and flawlessly bring a handful to their mouths. I tried and was clumsy, rice falling all over my sari. Without the chapati, that meal would have been a complete fail for me.

Sri Hari was fasting that day, and by serving our food, he could maintain a general busyness, a distraction that would keep his fingers from roaming over his hissing ribs. I suddenly thought of my grandfather. He was also tall, lean, and fasted for his spiritual life. In another life, he could have been a devout monk.

Sri Hari brought dessert next from a big steel tub: rice pudding, tiny butter cookies, and steaming hot chai. Sure, I'd had chai before in the States, but nothing prepared me for what I was about to sip. First, the heat of the milky tea, and then the hit of sweetness rolling around on my tongue with hints of cardamom. I couldn't stop sipping, and I emptied the small clear glass quickly. Sri Hari refilled my glass, and I was again in awe of the flavor. I couldn't have imagined then, as I gulped three cups hungrily, how significant that beverage would become for me. If only there were matted tea leaves on the bottom of that cup telling me my future.

It was such an unexpected feast. Hare Krishnas are known for their flavorful vegetarian food; hundreds of temples worldwide provide free meals every day, feeding hundreds of thousands. I learned Hare Krishnas feed thirty thousand schoolchildren a day in Bangalore and mobilize to feed millions during natural disasters.

A. C. Bhaktivedanta Swami, the creator of ISKCON, the International Society for Krishna Consciousness, declared that no one in a ten-mile radius of their temple would ever go hungry because food would always be free. Providing nutritious vegetation food became the glue for his spiritual movement, attracting hippies and counterculture Westerners throughout the sixties and seventies.

His story is miraculous. He came to the US in his seventies, with no money, on a steam ship. After having a heart attack on board and surviving, he managed to attract thousands of people to chant, sing, dance, meditate, and spread the love of Krishna consciousness. He was considered one of the great innovators by bringing the practice of ecstatic devotion from the fifteenth century to New York City and initiating a generation of dancing-in-the-street devotees that continues to grow to this day.

The conditions were ripe for his message of chanting instead of drugs, peace instead of war (attracting Vietnam War protesters), vegetarian food, and building an inner life. In the East Village, he was turning acidheads, potheads, bohemians, and hippies into devout monks. This one Indian man was then able to create a publishing empire distributing his translations and teachings from the Bhagavad Gita to English, and now there are more than 650 ISKCON temples and 115 ISKCON vegetarian restaurants, and it's the biggest organization in the world serving free food. Seems very Christ-like, and the kind of social service I liked in my spirituality.

In less than ten years, A.C. Bhaktivedanta's legacy was on par with Mahatma Gandhi's for spreading Hinduism, worship through dance and song, wholesome, hearty vegetation food, and making Krishna a global spiritual icon. When Steve Jobs was creating Apple and still sleeping on friends' floors, he went to the Hare Krishna temple every Sunday in California to have a free meal. He walked seven miles, and he later said it was his best meal of the week in those startup lean years.

With banana leaf plates spotless and when every last sip of water from the metal cups was gone, the boys went over to a wall of red drapes and pulled them open. Upon a small stage was a statue of Lord Krishna as a baby, painted all in blue. Then another curtain was pulled back, and an adult Krishna stood powerfully. The devotees lined up and moved closer to the statue, bowing and offering prayers and flowers. "This is *dharshan*," Sri Hari said, again in my ear. He wasn't shy to get close to me. Dharshan is the unveiling of a deity, but it's not just about seeing a statue; it's a sacred moment and considered reciprocal. So by viewing and praising and honoring a god, a goddess, or holy image, one is also blessed at the same time. This can also happen at home and is why so many Hindus have altars at home so the devotee and the deity can deepen prayer and connection.

I walked over to the stage and bowed down to pray clumsily. *Was I supposed kneel on the ground?* I didn't really know Krishna, so it felt a little strange, but consuming the body and blood of Christ also felt strange, and I had done it. I just started with *thank you* and then asked Krishna to guide me on my journey through India—to help me find my way and my purpose. *What was I supposed to be doing with my life? Why did I still feel like such an orphan?*

As I prayed, my mind wandered to my mother. Was it her and not the NPR reporter who had guided me to India? Perhaps, she had pulled some strings to get me to this place just as the drapes pulled open in front of me, cracking me open to find my way. She would have totally been the type to join the Hare Krishna movement in the seventies. It's exactly what she was searching for all those hitchhiking months. I believe she wanted me to start my journey through India with prayers in my heart.

Soon, we piled back in the short bus and headed to another temple.

This was a public temple and packed. We weaved through switchback lines like we were waiting for a Disneyland ride. Seeing the same faces winding around. They were all staring at me. But with smiles, not frowns. I kept my hair tucked under my scarf most of the day like Kerela advised, trying to pull off a Grace Kelly look like I was in a convertible on the French Riviera, but it was so fucking hot, the scarf was now wet with sweat, so I was an obvious foreigner.

Once we weaved our way through the incense-perfumed room, closer to the Krishna deity, I saw it was behind a silver-plated window with nine holes. Almost like a bulletproof shield. There was smoke and mirrors, so it felt like the statue was putting on a show. As I approached, a group of women asked to take my picture. Then another woman, then a group of men. The Hara

Krishna boys didn't like this. The white girl was becoming a distraction for the crowds of people and upstaging Krishna! I felt embarrassed to have so much attention to my whiteness, and that it was stopping the line from moving. The crowds grew bigger, and I was posing for endless photos.

I was smiling and posing, but inside, I was like, *Is this a fucking dream? How did I get here?* The only white woman surrounded by a light show from a god, but everyone wants my picture? With my sweaty pieces of hair framing my face? I missed my girlfriends in that moment. Someone to laugh with about how absurd this was. I would have bothered Sri Hari with my commentary, but he was all eyes closed, busy doing devotional stuff.

It was like the paparazzi, and I finally had to turn away and say no. But I did learn a little travel hack. If you're not blocking traffic or hindering prayers and puja in public, it's a beautiful opportunity to meet people and also ask to take their picture when they stop you for a picture. Win–win.

Kindness was sprinkled over me like the holy water dribbled onto our hands as we shuffled out. Then, Prasad was pressed into our hands on our way out. Unlike the dry, stick-to-the-roof-of-your-mouth communion wafer of my childhood, Prasad in India is sweet. This Holy Communion, blessed by the gods or priests and given after your prayers, is considered sacred. You are ingesting the blessings and oneness of God. It can be a sweet cookie, a sticky cake, a piece of banana or orange, or a sugar candy the size of a Tic-Tac. Monkeys sometimes end up with rotten teeth from scrounging around temples and eating discarded Prasad candy.

COILED COBRAS

A few days after the "Chant Hare Krishna and Be Happy" temple tour, Sri Hari and went to my kind of temple: the beach.

I was looking forward to an afternoon of skin-crisping sun and bathing in warm water. Sri Hari and I were dangling in and out of the line, waiting for the city bus. We couldn't stop flirting, and I knew being away from the watchful eyes of his Hare Krishna temple boys, we would finally kiss.

But it didn't start off very sexy. First, I was accosted by two teenage girls loosely holding wrapped-up babies. The girls came up behind me and began pinching the back of my arm, pulling quick angry tugs of flesh like a caliper measuring my arm fat index and said, "Money, money."

"Ouch," I yelled. And yes, it felt a little like they were also calling me fat. I felt bad seeing those babies limp in the heat. Too tired and hot to cry. I gave them a handful of rupees (probably five US dollars). They snatched the rupees, and then both moved closer and said, "More, more."

They'd seen my white face and knew I could give more. They knew disparity. They knew they had to bring in money or feel the pangs of hunger ripping through their tummies. I'm sure they would much rather be in school[3] and fed a school meal than lugging around babies begging for money in the scorching sun.

When we finally piled onto the sticky, crowded bus, I held the damp metal pole, trying not to think about the feces and germs chanting inside the metallic moisture. Meanwhile, prayer-bead-sized sweat rolled down my inner thigh, hidden under my long skirt, as the city bus curved through small villages. The bus driver's dashboard, splintering and cracking from the sun, was cluttered with altar objects—Shiva statues perched in every direction with

---

3   India has made significant strides in expanding access to education. In 2009, the Indian Parliament passed the Right to Education Act, which made it a human right for girls and boys to access free education between ages six and fifteen. For girls, it's still cloaked in obstacles to access. Girls are sixteen times more likely than boys to be out of school, and 40 percent of girls in India are not attending school due to poverty, caste, language, early marriage, childcare, home chores, village development, or male head of household disapproval.

fresh marigolds scattered over it all. The bus passed through a transparent cloud that smelled like dead bodies simmering in the sun, basted with a fishy marinade. Unlike a skunk smell, where I can find a manageable peppery center, this enveloping smell made me gag, and left even the locals grasping their shirts and saris to cover their noses.

When we arrived at the beach, Sri Hari and I were the only ones to get off the bus. It wasn't at all what I had expected. I knew it wasn't going to be Goa, thumping with electronic music, Europeans, flea markets, and artisan food trucks, but I expected a beachside café or a picnic table. Instead, there was nothing but a desolate beach. It was still exciting to see the Arabian Sea for the first time. Walking toward the water, I had to step around coils of human shit, like sleeping brown cobras.

We walked far down the beach to find water clear of floating cobras to find a place to set up our blanket. Then we walked close to the water's edge and let the waves roll over our toes in the ground-cardamom sand. The smell of salt in the air was intense, and I could taste it on my lips.

I thought of Gandhi and his first act of civil disobedience against the British, which ultimately led to India's independence. Gandhi and his followers marched over two hundred miles to the Arabian Sea to make salt from seawater, as was the practice in India before British colonizers made it illegal and instituted a salt tax on Indians. I wondered how far I was from that spot where Gandhi made history by standing up to colonizers to fight for independence and the freedom of natural resources.

We kept walking down the beach, grazing fingers, and Sri Hari took his sun-bleached peach scarf from around his neck and put it over us like a tent. We stared into each other's eyes and both leaned in to kiss—a passionate kiss that brought our bodies closer and closer together. This was not a kiss you'd expect from a holy man. Not just some little dainty kiss. He wasn't the naïve, inexperienced monk I had pictured. There was a real hunger in there, real passion, and the perfect amount of tongue—not a sloppy or sleepy tongue. The perfect make out kiss.

We went back and forth for hours—making out, rolling around, swimming, reading, and talking. The sun started to set; a creamy saffron sky was painted before us. The burning red globe slipped toward the water's edge on the horizon, a perfect red fireball jawbreaker sucked on by the world, and then was gone.

When we walked back toward the bus stop, it was dusk. We waited again at the bus stop with only men again. One man approached us and asked about my nationality. His teeth looked like they were bleeding, but I later learned it was from chewing betel leaves for their stimulant effects. It was four months after 9/11, and people were so kind when I said I was American. They would say, "Sorry for your loss. That was so tragic." I couldn't believe this because there was nonstop loss in India, with caste, gender, religious fights, and deaths daily, yet they were offering me condolences?

Then, another man in his early twenties joined, and another, and another. Where did they all come from? I was politely answering questions but felt encircled like I was in the temple. When the bus rolled up, Sri Hari gave a little flick of his hand to the group of men like the question-and-answer period was over. A few of them took a long last up-and-down stare of me, as if it were a final drag of a cigarette, and then slowly shuffled away. Everyone bustled to the front door. Sri Hari got on first, and before I could get on the step, two men grabbed me. I was pushed against the bus, and a wet mouth was forced over my mine. A snake tongue jabbed my clenched mouth for an instant before I pushed him away hard and ran up the bus steps saying, "Fuck you." I found Sri and started crying. It happened so fast, and tears came out of nowhere. I wanted to scream to everyone on the bus, "That guy just mouth-raped me!"

I kept telling myself it was just a silly kiss, trying to coax and calm myself, but it felt violent, scary, and toxic. I knew men were capable of being animals and monsters. I knew about the gang rapes in India. I was the lucky one. I'd escaped unscathed, unlike the thousands of girls and women raped in India each year. We'd all heard about the tragic, vile gang rapes and murders of a woman on a Delhi bus and a veterinarian on her way home from work, but most of the rapes that occur stay hidden inside, unspoken and never revealed.

India was starting to manhandle me. Just the sheer number of men on the streets was overwhelming. It was such a change from the US. So far, there was the assault from India on my senses, the sadness, the suffering, but also so much more of the sacred, sane, sweet, and calm. One moment I was high and blissed out on India, and the next, someone was shoving their tongue in my mouth. And not the tongue I liked in my mouth earlier that day.

CHAPTER 2

CO-CONSPIRATORS

Boulder, Colorado, 2003

"Every journey has a secret destination, of which the traveler is unaware."

—BUBER

The rosé-pink plus shape glared at me with certainty. It was a color I wanted to see in my wine glass, not on a pregnancy test. I held the flimsy stick, and heat rose to my face like a smack. Not one of shock as a naïve teenager who thought using a Today Sponge was enough to keep me from getting pregnant (it wasn't) but a whip of shame and anger that heading into my thirties I shouldn't have let this happen—again.

I had $300 in my checking account, a part-time job, and a new boyfriend of only six months. I hadn't even been home a year since my adventures in India and was still in a place of uncertainty. That path or purpose didn't reveal itself right after India as I had hoped.

When I'd found myself pregnant at seventeen, I immediately hauled the Yellow Pages from the closet, as heavy and dense as the Bible I was forced to read in my grandfather's study. I turned on Nirvana, and that angry roar filled me up as I flipped to the abortion services page. Like the "good news" in the gospels I learned so much about, the good news here was that abortion was legal, affordable, and accessible to a teenager without parental consent, my salvation. How devastating to think that thirty years later there are girls just like me in high school that don't have autonomy over their bodies and their futures.

While activists are responsible for progress, like expanding voting rights to women and African Americans, ending apartheid, making abortion legal and safe, and ensuring marriage equality, there are also activists on the other side working to limit rights, like access to abortion. I remember when I was in grade school the anti-choice activists arrived to town. They got all the churches to put up little white crosses, hundreds of them sticking out of the grass. It was a traveling antiabortion political statement for churches sent around the country, and it worked to convert many people. That one issue turned my yogurt-making, watercolor-painting, composting grandfather into a Focus on the Family, anti-choice, card-carrying Republican.

After my abortion in high school, I never had a minute of regret.

This time, though, I was an adult. This time, I had a master's degree. I had traveled, lived on my own, had a retirement account (that I couldn't touch until I was fifty-five, but still!). But my insides revolted. Pregnancy felt like a death. I wasn't ready to be a mother. I didn't have the desire, money, stability, career, life partner, or plan that I always assumed would come with a child.

I walked around for days after I took the pregnancy test, looking for a sign. Anything to tell me I was supposed to continue the pregnancy. Anything to show me that this was the right path—alarm bells, vivid dreams, a sudden influx of money. But there was nothing, and I couldn't will a miscarriage either. The only sign that arrived showed me that my checking account had just gone negative again. So I made the appointment.

First, the cold gel hit my belly to prepare me for the ultrasound to confirm I was six weeks pregnant, the collection of cells the size of a blueberry. I stared at the ceiling posters taped up for patients: snowcapped mountains, butterflies swarming an eruption of wildflowers.

"Oh look," the nurse said in a singsongy tone, "you're carrying twins!"

She couldn't mean me?

I lifted my head to catch her eyes. "Are you talking to *me*?" I hadn't been doing fertility treatments, and twins are not in my family. *Two?* How could this be possible? I was in complete shock. I still didn't believe she was talking to me as she was oddly smiling and pointing at the screen. Didn't she realize I was there for an abortion?

You mean my oh-fuck-I'm-knocked-up is now oh-fuck-I'm-knocked-up-with-twins? I couldn't handle having one; how could I handle having two?

Having an unplanned pregnancy was already shrouded in stress. But then, finding out the pregnancy was unexpected twins? That was going to war without ever doing basic training. Tears fell down the corners of my eyes uncontrollably. Something inside of me was breaking. Was this the alarm bell? Was this the vivid dream?

I left in shock with two blueberries in my body.

That night, I dreamed I was driving fast down a muddy road with cavernous potholes when suddenly I hit two bodies. I got out and saw they were not human bodies but black snakes. I got back in the car, and suddenly a third life-size snake came to the driver's window, toward my face. I didn't flinch. It came closer like it was going to swallow me up, and I closed my eyes and let out the breath I had been holding. I felt the snake circling my head and gulping my body like the elephant in *Le Petit Prince*, visible in the boa constrictor's body. I relaxed into that dark corridor of the snake. I waited, trusted, and didn't allow fear to overcome me. The snake finished its test, retreated, and slid out the window. I drove on.

I started to see the two beings within me choosing each other and choosing me, co-conspirators bending my arm to let go of my fear of being a mother. Two beings were pushing me into the unknown dark waters of trust, and in time my heart opened to them and pregnancy. I was scared like that snake enveloping me, but it wouldn't kill me, right? But then it did kill my mother. That was the deeper fear swirling around inside of me: Will it end up being my demise? Will I too die early in motherhood?

One hundred practical reasons pulled me to that appointment, but now I heard something else. *You will survive this and be fiercer. This is your path, and you will be supported.* There is a death with pregnancy, but it's a death of the old self. Surrender was my only option.

I still had these fleeting thoughts of leaving, running away from reality, as if I could be a man with a choice to walk away. But they were in *my* body. I couldn't run away, and I couldn't hide. There was no escape. I had to face this myself. I had to be loyal to what I knew had to happen now, even when I wasn't *feeling* knowing. Maybe I could look at motherhood not with fear, but as another type of adventure.

After the shock wore off and acceptance slid in, I pulled myself up out of denial and dove into pregnancy. Vitamins, yoga, herbs, pregnancy massages, daily walks, juicing, journaling, and sleeping. I took care of my body as a full-time job. My boyfriend, Judd, proposed. I didn't want to get officially married, nor did I believe in the idea of forever with one person (or want to believe in that because I like to keep my options open), but I also didn't want to do this alone. Plus, we were in love. Maybe that was enough? He was Jewish and we spent our Friday nights at hippie Shabbat dinners singing songs, wine dripping over the cup on the plate to signify our abundance. We did have fun together, and we did love to laugh together. Maybe that would be enough?

Judd also brought a son I fell in love with to the relationship. A four-year-old boy named Moe, with a squeaky, high voice, wispy thin white hair, and big, startled-looking blue eyes. So from my limited time with this man, he seemed like he was into the fathering role and was very loving with Moe. I was starting to feel excited about building a family together. I loved putting Moe to bed and reading him stories, taking him to the park and singing songs with him in the car. Maybe I would be a good stepmom and mom after all.

We agreed to a commitment ceremony but not a legal marriage. We could both commit to try this new life of parenting together and see how it went. I had known him for less than a year, not good odds for a marriage, let alone even the odds of dating him another year. But I could give it the old college try.

We called it a commitment ceremony on the postcards we sent out (some friends wondered if I was marring a woman) and it was outside in the mountains with friends, music, poetry, and a bonfire. We brought in the four directions, Judd wrote a song and sang it to me, friends read poems—all under a huppah. I was nauseous and couldn't drink, so not the most storybook wedding day, but many of my friends came from out of town and we sipped chocolate malts getting ready, my favorite ice cream treat.

As I reached the eighth month of pregnancy, I was enormous; the babies pushed my breasts up toward my chin. I could have balanced a platter on them. A friend organized a blessing circle for me. A blessingway is a Navajo tradition to celebrate a woman's rite of passage into motherhood and invoke positive blessings for the birthing process and the mothering process. It's about nurturing the mother, honoring the woman, coaxing out fear, and filling her up with peace and hope about the new transition to motherhood. They arrived with candles, each one to light the long, dark corridor of labor. They came with sage, sweetgrass, crystals, flowers, incense, gifts, and food, and they surrounded me with love. A circle of beautiful women braided my hair and massaged my arms and swollen feet in rose petal warm water.

My friends shared poems, blessings, anecdotes, and songs. They stuffed me with homemade soups, pasta, empanadas, and pastries. Then, I pulled out the same book my mother used during her street proselyting sessions and read a Kahlil Gibran[4] essay to honor my mother and to remind me what I was doing—allowing those babies to come through me.

NICU

My water broke a week later, five weeks before my due date. I wanted a natural birth, and luckily, they came pounding at the door, so it was natural, but I was whisked to the hospital for safety. When my twins arrived, they looked like tiny alien babies. Blue veins pushed through their parchment-paper skin. Their eyes clenched and their mouths pursed as if they were awoken too early. A bright interrogation light blasted on them before their pupils had acclimated. The incubators radiated them with

---

4   This is the complete Kahlil Gibran script: "Your children are not your children. They are the sons and daughters of life's longing for itself. They come through you, but not from you. And though they are within you, yet they belong not to you. You may give them your love, but not your thoughts, for they have their thoughts. You may house their bodies, but not their souls, for their souls dwell in the house of tomorrow—which you cannot visit, not even in your dreams. You may strive to be like them but seek not to make them like you. For life goes not backward nor tarries with yesterday. You are the bows from which your children are the living arrows sent forth. The archer sees the mark upon the path of the infinite."

life. Their breath, like tiny sighs puttering, so faint only a stethoscope could decipher. Veda was three and a half pounds, and an hour later, Ryzen was born at four and a half pounds—a massive chunk, comparatively.

I only got to glance at them before they were whisked away to the neonatal intensive care unit (NICU). The first time I really saw them, they were cloaked in equipment. Plastic tubes were in their noses and then taped to their thin cheek skin; IV lines poked their tiny Barbie-doll arms, and their blood pressure was monitored with miniature cuffs around their ankles, like they were on house arrest, while bili lights in the incubator treated them for jaundice.

Their dad and I lived in the hospital with them for a month. It was a blur of lactation consultants stuffing my nipples into small baby faces, almost drowning them in my flesh. I fed them every three hours like clockwork—eight times within twenty-four hours and pumping after each feeding to increase my milk supply. I was being milked—like a cow.

I would stare out the window of the hospital after my 6:00 a.m. feeding, just as the sun was torching the tops of the trees, changing colors while the industrial machine was pulling milk out of me with a loud "whah…whah…whah" rhythm and think about my mother. When her water broke, she didn't get rushed to the hospital like me—instead, her friends started arriving for a party. They brought food, played instruments, or walked my mother up and down the stairs. While I was so thankful for the brilliant medical intervention I had, it felt sterile and detached, and smelled of disinfectant. I was envious of my mother having a home birth with a potluck full of people.

I didn't learn my birth story until I tracked down my mother's friends when I was in my twenties. Before the waywardness of hitchhiking, my mother lived in a community of hippies in

Glenwood Springs, Colorado. This was before cafés hummed with motion or fleece-frenzy climbing gear stores spotted Main Street as they do today. Glenwood Springs in the early seventies was still the sometimes-motionless jewel, briefly glimmering and then abruptly disappearing into the mountains off Interstate 70. You could miss it if you didn't notice the steam coming off the largest mineral hot springs in the world or the bitter stench of sulfur wafting from the vapor caves.

My mother was unwavering about having a home birth. While her mother had an epidural and didn't breastfeed any of her children ("That's just what we did in my day," my grandmother would remind me), my mother wanted it natural.

Mountain passes closed that night, and snow curtained parked cars the December morning I was born. I was eight pounds and healthy. But when the placenta wouldn't budge, and my mother's body began to burn with fever, some of her friends drove her to the hospital while I stayed back at the house with the others. Independent my very first day.

A friend of my mother's brought me to visit her later that night. She recounted the story of how we roamed the hallways. I was concealed like contraband and swaddled in blankets. We found the maternity ward, and she cradled me close to the window, showing me a baby who couldn't roam free like me. I couldn't help but smile, knowing that the first day of my life was filled with freedom, foreshadowing my lifelong need for independence. Perhaps it was those first few hours that wired in me the knowledge that ultimately, I would have to take care of my destiny and myself.

Just like my mother, I, too, ended up sick, burning with an infection. Luckily, I was already living in the hospital, and they realized I still had some of the placenta rotting inside of me. It was Halloween day, and a friend had brought me a wig that morning with a smoothie. So when they wheeled me down to surgery for a D&C, I was wearing a black Elvira wig. Trying to make some fun in that stark environment.

When Ryzen and Veda were finally released from the hospital, we settled into our A-frame cabin in Nederland, a little mountain town above Boulder. I could finally hold them close without worrying about the lines, beeps, or tubes. I could sleep next to them without nurses standing over me. But soon, reality hit. I was a new mother *with* twins, but *without* help from a mother. I wanted those watchful nurses back to help me. Or I wanted that bread pudding I could order off the dessert menu in the middle of the afternoon at the hospital. Thankfully, Judd was there to help, and those first few months we were up together every night doing feedings and changings. But he wasn't making me dessert.

I still felt alone, in the middle of winter, with these two new beings. I cried most days in the beginning. I'd stare at the shriveled damp leaves peeking out under the snow outside. Snapping twigs, lifeless soil, and a dusty gray sky hung heavy on a sleep-deprived postpartum mom. And then the wind began, whipping the house with her long, fierce hair, stinging my soul. The house wheezed and creaked for what felt like months.

While Veda and Ryzen were becoming chunkier to cuddle, with wide eyes the color of the sea and strands of white hair, they were also colicky. It usually began with Veda. She cursed in tongues, wails, and screams, with claws of fire reaching out of her tiny little mouth, and then moved to a grunting pattern of noises, sometimes for hours. Ryzen joined in for a cacophony of cries, trying to eclipse her rage but unable to sustain her force. I tried changing my diet, cutting out garlic, onions, milk, spices, soy, beans, wheat, eggs, nuts, rice. That didn't do anything but make me crave food and resentful I couldn't have eggs and toast. I gave them colicky tinctures, moved their little legs around trying to release gas, and took them outside on walks, but nothing worked.

My tears dropped all over that house in the first year. I cried while washing the dishes, scrubbing the floor, and stoking the fire. Sometimes I cried while hiding in the shower so their father wouldn't hear. Other days I couldn't conceal the oily tears dripping down my face as I held my babies and tried to feed them both in what is called the "football hold"—two baby footballs tucked under my arms and clutched next to my bursting breasts. It never worked. Veda would need to be burped while Ryzen would drink too much and then projectile hurl milk across the room.

During those hard months, I thought about how easy my mother had it with one child. I romanticized all the things she would be doing for me if she were still alive. Helping with the babies, baking, cleaning, doing laundry, massaging my feet, teaching me what to do—all the things I imagined mothers do after their daughters give birth. All the grief I thought I had resolved about my mother surfaced. Psychologists call it STUGs— subsequent, temporary upsurge of grief. I couldn't mourn as a motherless mother until I *was* a motherless mother.

When Ryzen and Veda napped, I found solace in chai. I leaned over a pot of boiling tea, letting the steam vapors beat up on my face like an intense facial, while the spices bloomed around me—and I was transported back to India. No longer stranded in a drafty mountain A-frame with colicky twins erupting in wails or dealing with diaper blowouts smeared up backs, but sitting with a band of Hare Krishnas in temples sipping sweet chai. I didn't know I would stumble upon being an entrepreneur as I shredded fresh ginger into the twirling tea, each ingredient a prayer. But there it was on my lips: *India in a cup.* Even though I didn't yet know what it meant, I knew I was on to something because I smiled. This idea of escaping to India in my mind, and in my kitchen, made me feel free and hopeful.

CHAPTER 3

UNEXPECTED
ENTREPRENEUR

Boulder, Colorado, 2005

"The most difficult thing is the decision to act. The rest is merely tenacity."

—AMELIA EARHART

reating a recipe from all the chai I had experienced during my three-month trip to India was an escape. Tinkering with it was just as enjoyable as savoring it or feeling the much-needed caffeine jolt from being a sleep-deprived new mother in a trance most mornings. It became a meditation for me: my mortar and pestle grinding away at cardamom seeds. Then the olfactory floodgate of memories in India, bringing me back to that sandy cardamom beach. I experimented with different sugar levels, distinct spices, diverse teas, and endless variations of steep times. I didn't want subtle spice; instead, I went for super-power and juiced ginger, adding an unapologetic amount of it to the swirling black tea. That recipe was my hobby, my escape, my daily dose of caffeine, and my salvation. A type of silent meditation. Busying my hands and mind by making chai batches saved me that year.

A year after my twins were born, I was still in that mountain A-frame, but we were broke. I had walking babies at that point—or more like two wobbling drunks. They stumbled, scaled furniture, crashed into each other, and wrestled. They started to get cuts and bruises, and I worried about not having any health insurance—no money if one of them was hurt or became seriously ill. They had grown on breast milk, bananas, avocados, and oatmeal, and those tiny preemies now had rolls of fat and giant heads. We snuggled and explored in nature, and I was happy, but my vision for my life was obscured.

Their father was the classic ADHD/pot-smoking procrastinator. While he loved the twins and helped as much as he could, he wasn't interested in working for money. We began to fight more about the inequities in labor with the kids, around the house, and him not financially providing. I couldn't even afford a babysitter or a haircut, let alone the thought of the future with having two children growing bigger.

I knew the first year was so important, and I wanted all my energy to be on Ryzen and Veda. But that year was up, and I had cabin fever. I couldn't sit by and hope he would suddenly have ambition. I had to pull myself away from the Mountain Mama phase and into the Mama Bear phase of financially taking care of my children by myself.

Meanwhile, my good friend in Sweden was getting a monthly check as a new mom. A mother's stipend for taking off that first year to stay home with her child. A paycheck just for her to use for a babysitter, food, a haircut, or a new coat. Men can also take advantage of the parenting stipend the second year if mothers want to go back to work. If only mothers in the US could get a stipend for their work in creating the next generation of citizens.

The unpaid work that women do equals $10 trillion a year globally in lost wages. Can you fathom our country if women (or men) were paid a monthly stipend to raise children, build communities, cook, clean, educate, support, or care for the elderly? Working moms basically do two full-time jobs simultaneously and only get paid (eighty-three cents on the male dollar) for one. I was doing everything at home, but the designated earner was not, so I had to make a change and do both.

I learned early that economic mobility for women bought freedom. My grandmother received an allowance every week from my grandfather for groceries. Even the word *allowance* sounds so demeaning. I knew if she went over that amount at the grocery store because she would pull on her lower lip and nervously tell me to put back the fun items: cereal, English muffins, ginger ale, or hot dogs. If my grandmother wanted something extra, she would have to sit down with my grandfather and ask in advance for an increased allowance. An additional thirty dollars was scrutinized if she wanted to get her hair "frosted." I understand, they were on a one-income budget, I just didn't want to live like that. But my grandmother was also enterprising[5] and would sit down at the kitchen table every week and cut out coupons—frequently waving one in her hand and saying in her high-pitched voice, "entering another sweepstakes!" She worked the sweepstakes circuit like a bookie. She won a La-Z-boy chair, a television, a VCR, an embroidered love seat, a weekend getaway, and countless other free products. Those were all *her* earnings. She also deserved a mother stipend (and grandmother stipend) that I'm sure she would have joyfully spent on herself, her community, and her family.

---

5   When my grandmother was in her sixties, she decided to get a part-time job at AAA and had a little more economic freedom. She worked the TripTik desk. The actual person to plan out your road trip with a fat blue highlighter on a flip map. She was what is now Google Maps.

I watched this growing up and vowed never to depend on a man or a partner regarding money or spending. I told myself I wouldn't ever live like that. Yet there I was, putting back corn chips and avocados at our local co-op when my credit card was declined because the kids' dad wasn't working again. It's not like there wasn't work or endless paid opportunities. He just didn't have the motivation or drive to work. But I did.

My first job was a paper route at eleven years old. Then on to a chocolate store, a French bakery, a pizza shop—where, at sixteen, I realized I could abandon the hot ovens, burned fingers, and squirting greasy flavored butter on crusts to whiz away with the freedom and tips as a pizza delivery girl.

I had tasted the freedom of making and spending my own money. Even in times when I couldn't find a job, I created one. I never went to massage school, but I did start a business called Lucid Massage. I borrowed a friend's massage table and put up red flyers advertising in-home massages around town with tear-off sections on the bottom with my phone number. The worst part was when I'd take down the sheet on the massage table and discover men with hair patches strewn across their backs, glaring brown tufts sticking out from shoulder blades, or long, wispy, salt-and-pepper strands. I knew my organic argan-coconut oil blend would soon be tangled up in those long shreds of hair. But I ignored my gag reflex and dug my thumbs into their muscles, for money.

It wasn't the paper or pizza delivery, the French pastry, or the massage techniques that I learned from these jobs. It was hustle. I learned to MSH (make shit happen). I learned how to sell, how to market, and how to never give up. I had learned early that I would be the only person to improve my life, and I wasn't about to stop leaning on myself now.

As Ryzen and Veda's second Christmas approached (the first one was shrouded in newborn colicky stress), their dad still didn't have a consistent income. We didn't have money to spend on Christmas gifts, so I decided to give my liquid chai as my offering to friends and neighbors. I looked around and saw eight Mason jars on our counter filled with dried goods. I put oats, flour, wheat germ, dried cherries, coconut, and almonds on a baking sheet with butter and honey and made granola, and then I washed out the Mason jars to use for chai. I brewed a big batch of tea and added the fresh ginger juice, cardamom, clove, star anise, and sugar, letting it simmer and stew all day. I found flocked and patterned papers from an old wallpaper book I'd saved for making collages and began to make labels for the jars full of chai, using Hafiz, Kabir, and Rumi quotes, depending on who I was giving it to and what poem struck me. I felt proud that I was giving a part of me, a part of my experience in India. In Joseph Campbell's book *The Hero's Journey*, after the call to adventure, there's a phase called "returning with the elixir." While I didn't bring back an actual tea or recipe, I was bringing back what inspired me in India and sharing that.

Something happened a week after Christmas: some of those Mason jars showed up on my counter, empty with notes asking for more chai. The first one came from a neighbor who left a five-dollar bill—another from a friend who gave me a twenty.

How sweet, I thought. *They know I'm strapped for cash and are trying to help me.*

Then a few phone calls came from other friends also wanting chai refills. It hit me: *maybe there were more twenty-dollar bills around the corner if I made more chai and built something more significant than just brewing a batch for myself. Maybe this could be a side hustle?* And then the big thought—*or maybe this is the purpose I've been searching for?* I held the empty Mason jar from my neighbor and read the Hafiz quote I had attached to it a week earlier:

"You carry all the ingredients to turn your existence into joy.

Mix them! Mix them!"

It was a message to me now. The messages were there all along. I'd been carrying them and collecting them throughout my life, like the quotes and flock paper. I had it right in front of me. I was overflowing with all the ingredients I'd been collecting, all the nuggets of wisdom, all the letting go, all the listening, all the jobs, all the experiences, and all the influences to start a chai company. I had the answer for joy within me.

Those friends and neighbors were my first focus group, but I needed a real test market. If I could convince just one café to carry my chai, then I could make that my test market and learn how this would all work. But before this, I needed to understand pricing and the competition, so I traveled from the mountains down to Boulder and did some reconnaissance, with Ryzen and Veda chirping away in the back seat.

What cafés and restaurants could I approach? What were they serving for chai? How much were they charging? I tried everything from syrup chai (a chai-flavored syrup without tea or real spices, just flavors) similar to the pump syrup chai you get at Starbucks, to chai powders (again, flavors and powdered spices with dried milk powder), to the more common national brands. I couldn't drink any of them. In a café near the University of Colorado called Burnt Toast, I asked the owner if she'd be willing to try my homemade chai. "Sure," she said with enthusiasm.

The next day, I drove down the mountain and headed to Burnt Toast with my first samples. It was one of those blinding sunny mornings after a spring snowstorm. The sun seemed to ricochet off the bright white snow while heavy, wet snow fell from trees abruptly in sheets. The chai was still warm from my stove, and I held my hand over two glass Mason jars sitting next to me in the front seat and said a prayer. I asked that it warm people and fill them with joy and the peace I found in India. I also asked that it provide some funds for me.

The owner, a woman named Margo, called me the next day. "We all loved it. It's the best chai I've ever had, and my baristas have already finished both jars. We'll take three gallons a week." She didn't even ask about the pricing.

Okay. This is it. I can't turn back once I start gaining customers. Do I want to start a chai company? I thought. I looked up and asked, *Do I really want to start a chai company?* The answer hit me without me thinking: *Yes. Do it!* It was something inside—my gut, my grit, or my guides. That's how it all began.

I wish I could say founding my company was purely philanthropic. It was far more about survival and seeing a way to create income and bring my kids and me into a more financially stable situation. I used to think I was an accidental entrepreneur. But then I realized my entrepreneurial spirit, or my *dharma*, my truth, had always been with me, swirling around inside, delivering those pizzas and giving those massages—percolating all those years for this very moment.

LIQUID GOLD

I dove headfirst into the unknown of starting a beverage company. It couldn't be that hard, could it? You have to have some naiveté launching a business. If I'd known how hard it was going to be, how many people I would have to manage and coddle, beg, plead, pay off, focus on, fire, mediate within legal battles, scratch my way up, and fight as I pushed a rock uphill for decades, I would never have started that day. But I didn't know, so I happily plunged into entrepreneurship, completely unaware.

The word *chai* means "tea," and tea is the number two drink in the world, behind water. To determine the tea I would source for my business, I went to an expert. I met with an Indian tea importer to learn about different tea offerings and finalize my recipe for scale. His name was Vishnu, and he had big glossy brown eyes and a protruding, hard belly that he rested his crossed arms on. I spent an afternoon doing cuppings and tried dozens of varietals of black, green, and herbal teas. "Can you taste the cherry?" he asked with a slight head wobble. Like a seasoned sommelier, he called out undertones and subtleties of the tea—notes of lemongrass, butter, herbs, and raspberry.

Like wine, astringency is an essential characteristic of tea. I didn't want anything too bitter or too cottonmouth-after-smoking-marijuana. I tried many until I found a bright version that only with my tea sommelier hat on, creative imagination, or wishful thinking revealed whiskey notes. It was a black tea from Assam[6] known for its hearty malt flavor, which works well with milk and sugar. It's in most English Breakfast and Early Grey blends.

It was not an overpowering tea because, for my recipe, the tea was just the base; it wasn't supposed to be the main character. It shouldn't upstage the ginger and other spices, which were the celebrities and, as such, needed the spotlight.

The discovery of tea comes from the story of an accidental encounter in China over five thousand years ago. The legend is it was either a Buddhist monk or an emperor that discovered a green tea leaf had floated into their cup of boiling water and,

---

6   This is the region in Northeast India studded with lush hills, ridges, streams, a tropical river valley, and mountains on all sides but the west. Assam is the only region in India with indigenous tea plants, Camellia sinensis growing wild and first discovered in 1823 (or first documented) by Robert Bruce; then, after his death, his brother learned how to propagate, cultivate, and produce black tea from these green tea leaves. It's thought that the green leaves could have been consumed prior to the production of tea as a food for nutritional value.

after drinking it, felt awakened and alert. In the monk's story, it helped him stay focused during meditation, so he shared it with his students so they could stave off sleeping during meditation. In the emperor story, he thought it would make his soldiers attentive and energized, and he gave it to them before going into battle. This is where the term *tea mind* comes from. Being clear, focused, and having a jolt of clean energy. We now know the evidence of the health benefits in tea: it's antioxidant-rich, full of L-theanine and caffeine, boosts heart health, and reduces the risk of stroke and cancer. I'd like to believe it was the former monk story that made this discovery. Don't we have enough testosterone-induced war stories in our history? But knowing our history is deficient of stories from women, it seems more likely to me a woman would have been preparing hot water and discovered the tea leaf floating and steeping in the water.

When I was sipping homemade chai in temples or on the streets of India, I assumed chai would also have a sweet origin story. I imagined it came from a long Ayurvedic[7] lineage as a healing tonic in India—an elixir of spices and tea for immunity. Unfortunately, chai has an unsavory origin story in India, as Vishnu explained. I was shocked to learn that the chai culture that is so beautiful and pure in India was actually rooted within capitalism, control, and colonialism.

The popularity of chai in India actually evolved from a marketing campaign, a surplus of tea, a company hungry for profits, and a history rife with theft. The East India Company (formed initially to compete with Spain and Portugal in the lucrative textile and later spice trade) was a British corporation far more

---

7   The word Ayurveda comes from the Sanskrit words ayur ("life") and veda ("knowledge") and is an ancient health tradition practiced since 6000 BCE. Ayurveda combines herbal and mineral compounds in a holistic approach using roots, leaves, seeds, and diet to address one's constitution—their pitta, vata, and kapha.

powerful than any government. As historian and writer William Dalrymple writes, "It was the first global corporate power that controlled both the economics and politics of half the world and exerted more control than Google, Tesla, Facebook, ExxonMobil, and Microsoft combined."

Not only was the East India Company responsible for dominating trade, commerce, and governance in India—they were also the source of those 342 boxes of tea dumped into Boston Harbor in 1773. It was shocking to learn it wasn't the British government that completely colonized India; rather, for a century, a British business controlled many parts of India. The East India Company was setting up alliances with Indian kings and regional leaders, and hired Indian mercenaries to protect all their assets and profitable trade channels. Arming them with weapons to protect their tea, opium, and exports—later to fight against and kill their own people. These corporate armies were double the size of the actual British government army. It's strange to think of the power we've allowed businesses to wield. Multinational corporations overthrowing governments for profits, arming citizens and hiring mercenaries, and today, companies like SpaceX similarly exploring and then potentially exploiting new frontiers.

The more I learned about tea, the more its complicated history unfolded. In its two-hundred-year unbridled company history, the East India Company had been selling opium[8] to China (from poppies grown in India) to pay for their tea. China had a monopoly on tea at the time—it was the only country to grow, pick, process, sell, and export tea, or as they called it, liquid jade.

---

8   India was the largest producer of opium, controlled by the East India Company monopoly, with China at the time being the largest consumer. Today, they are the largest producer of opium gum sold to pharmaceutical companies, but Afghanistan is the largest overall producer (the sale of opium helps to fund the Taliban), and holds an 85 percent global monopoly on all opium, with large concentrations of heroin laboratories and end consumers all through Europe, the Americas, Russia, Iran, and Africa.

But after the opium wars, which were fought over two flowers (poppies and *Camellia sinensis*), the East India Company stole[9] tea seeds from China to cultivate in India, which created a sensation for the company and unleashed the Indian tea rush. Just like our gold rush, men dreamed of fortunes made by cultivating tea from stolen seeds and sometimes stolen land (*loot* was the first recorded English word in India) to quench the thirst of the growing demand for tea in Great Britain and beyond. During the next four decades, thousands of acres were cleared and millions of seedlings planted in India.

Indians didn't drink tea, and all the tea produced there was exported, that is until the first marketing operation, or what we would later call in marketing a "drink occasion" campaign. But their attempts to foster a domestic market for tea faced a significant obstacle: it was the beginning of the Indian independence movement, and Indians viewed tea as a foreign, exploitative commodity. Gandhi labeled tea the "blood of the peasants of Assam." This was the drink of profiteers, greedy capitalists, and the drink of colonizers pillaging the land and mechanizing production for profits. It was also considered a vice like cigarettes and whiskey. Just like Ted Lasso, many Indians first thought of tea like hot brown water.

But when international tea prices dropped sharply in 1932, the Indian Tea Market Expansion Board started one of the most extensive marketing campaigns in Indian history. With a surplus of more than a hundred million pounds of tea, they saw the 350

---

9 It was a Scottish botanist named Robert Fortune, working for the East India Company, who became known as the greatest trade secrets thief of all time. He traveled by boat disguised in Chinese clothes and survived illness and pirate attacks to steal tea seeds from China that were then planted in India. He was also responsible for bringing certain roses, peonies, the bleeding heart, azaleas, and the kumquat to the West. Before working for the East India Company, he was hired by the US to develop tea plantations in the South. He brought another batch of stolen seeds and set up his R&D farms in Georgia, Florida, and South Carolina, but the Civil War halted that work, and the only surviving tea garden from that experimental time is in Summerville, Georgia.

million Indians as "thirsty throats awaiting initiation." This was the beginning of a grand marketing campaign and the introduction of tea to Indians.

Academic Philip Lutgendorf described advertisements that proclaimed tea would make Indians more alert, energetic, and even punctual (read: better workers). Tea propagandists, or what we now call brand ambassadors or "social influencers" in marketing, were dispatched in the hundreds, sometimes in motorized tea vans, equipped to dispense millions of free samples of tea. Posters created by commercial artists popped up all around the country of people drinking chai with the taglines "fights fatigue" or "healthy" printed in multiple languages.

Brooke Bond and Lipton sold their tea at subsidized prices so Indians could afford it when they were starting to form a habit. Then, they came out with the tea bags to give as samples for further drug-pushing tactics. Another approach to foster addiction urged factory owners and office managers to set up free or subsidized canteens on their premises and offer an afternoon tea break to keep workers alert and attentive. Perhaps this is where Google got the idea of setting up onsite canteens with everything a worker could need to not go home.

The campaign also targeted women.[10] It wasn't Ayurveda practitioners or family recipes passed down through the ages that popularized chai, but corporate greed. Indians did put their fla-

---

10 These advertisements featured middle-class women, aristocratic women, and movie stars, showing it was the proper thing to consume tea for health, to reenergize and savor. With the debates around self-rule and independence, some argued that India wasn't ready due to the uneducated and oppressed station of women. Tea was touted as a vehicle for the women's progressive movement and an empowering tool for intelligent, modern homemakers who understood the importance of good nutrition and daily teatime. In addition, the tea propaganda efforts adopted the independence movement's nationalist rhetoric to champion tea as India's national beverage that could potentially unify India's diverse religious, linguistic, and caste groups. Women did pass down their specific masala chai recipes to their daughters after the 1950s. During the first formal arranged marriage family meetings (which is still the norm in India but changing with the rise of online dating and choosing partners outside of family and caste connections), families are served chai and potential suitors are known to consider the recipe when deciding on a match. If someone is raised drinking sweet chai, then being served spicy chai could be a sign that the potential marriage is not a fit.

vorful culinary spin on the tea and added spices to create masala chai. Once accepted, Indians began drinking and experimenting with different variations, and, over time, chai became a place of pride as the national drink, as it is today. In less than fifty years, it became the largest tea-drinking country in the world.

SOURCING

Learning the sordid past of tea made it even more important to know the origins of tea. Tea comes from lush farms, where women carefully pluck green leaves by hand, and then it's sent to a processing plant to become black tea. I wanted to make sure the black tea I used was fair trade and organic. I wasn't going to build a tea company on the backs of women tea pickers in India who were not getting a fair wage.

Fair trade means tea plantation workers are given a livable wage and access to healthcare, education, paid time off, and bonus checks. Fair trade means the owners share the profits with all the workers, and fair-trade farms also receive millions of dollars to invest in community health clinics and schools. Higher wages ensure that women and children have better lives and entire communities flourish.

I also insisted that all my ingredients were organic. Organic agriculture builds healthy soil and helps to combat climate change. It helps to keep our oceans, lakes, and rivers clean of pesticides. It supports good health, but more importantly, it doesn't expose women to pesticides that lead to cancer. Using organic and fair-trade ingredients wasn't about slapping a certified logo on my product. It was about a principled stance on the kind of society we all want to live in. It meant paying a premium, but I didn't even consider doing otherwise.

In medieval times, spices were used as currency and sometimes considered contraband. The hunger for spices galvanized countries, built fortunes, and subjugated natives. Some of the most expensive spices extracted from Asia (and then exported by the East India Company and the Portuguese) were ginger, cloves, pepper, and cardamom—all ingredients I was using in my chai recipe.

If the tea leaves are the base, full of antioxidants and caffeine, ginger was the linchpin. When simmering the ginger root wasn't fiery enough for me, I juiced the ginger. I wanted what is called *agni*, or fire, to be in every cup of my chai. The smell of ginger was intoxicating, and the taste alone would burn you up, but the bright yellow shots of ginger were the star of the show. Ginger jolts the senses alive and boosts digestion and the immune system. It helps with nausea and migraines and works to break up inflammation in the body associated with cancer.

I first bought organic ginger root from a natural foods market in Boulder. Then the local Asian market. But soon, I was buying up all their weekly organic ginger and needed a consistent supply at wholesale pricing. I found an importer in California who was buying organic ginger root from Peru. They sent me a sample, and when I snapped it in half, a bright yellow, juicy center blared out in all her glory. This was the gold—soon to be made into liquid gold in my juicer. The body was like milk and the color of bright lemons. That ginger was sowed, harvested, and packed in the Peruvian Amazon rainforest, which had the ideal soil and climate for organic ginger, and the farm provided fixed hours of work for women with children and families, medical stipends, and paid time off. It was an alternative job from working in nearby farms growing coca[11] that will be processed into cocaine. Again,

---

[11] On its own this is a beautiful crop and has been offering sustenance for communities in Peru for 8,000 years. Chewing the coca leaf or making tea provides a stimulant and energy similar to coffee and was a tradition and everyday nutritious part of the South American diet. It was the basis, with the kola nut, for Coca-Cola, but with the production of cocaine and the demand so high all across the world for this export, women working on coca farms preferred the more reliable and safer work on ginger plantations.

I was proud to find a supplier that paid women workers well and had their best interests in mind.

I wasn't going to Americanize my chai with cinnamon, nutmeg, vanilla, or honey; I didn't want the traditional chai essence people call "Christmas chai" or "pumpkin pie spice chai." It had to dance in your mouth and throat, warm you up from the inside out, and stay true to my Mason jar samples of bringing forth India in a cup. Not syrupy nutmeg and vanilla chai in a cup.

Cardamom has a sweet, rich fragrance and is in the same family as ginger. Some of the best cardamom seeds are found in the cloudy forests of Guatemala, where farmers pick cardamom pods by feel and experience. They should be soft to the touch, like an olive, but not too dry. More than half of the world's cardamom comes from Central America, and it is the third most expensive spice globally, behind saffron and vanilla, due to the labor-intensive process. Cardamom was my beloved in the masala mix. *Masala* means "a combination of spices," and for my chai, I used cardamom, black pepper, clove, and star anise.

And finally, sugar. My sweet, sweet sister sugar. Oh, I know, it's the new smoking, the new sitting, *and* the new heroin all at once. We're bombarded with the afflictions that come from sugar and told to hide from those calories, carbs, and curses. But it balances out flavors, and it coats your mouth with joy.

The first refined sugar was created in India 2,500 years ago, and sugarcane is the third most valuable crop in the world. I played around extensively with the amount of sugar because I didn't want a saccharine-syrupy, heavy-handed sugar hiding the complex flavors of cardamom, ginger, and tea. Besides, the competitors were already doing this—some chai options at Starbucks and other coffee chains had sixty-five to ninety-five grams of sugar per serving. I bought bags and bags of evaporated cane juice (which might sound healthy but it's basically sugar) and went to work on the amount and sourcing. I soon found some organic and fair-trade sugar from Brazil that was the best price and quality.

THE MARK

When I had a recipe and sourcing finalized, I needed a name and a brand. I've seen hundreds of companies spend $5,000 to $80,000 (and larger consumer package goods brands spend upward of $200,000) on an exercise in letting someone else come up with the soul of the brand. To be honest, I probably would have done that if I'd had the money. It sounded fun to bring others into the energy of helping to create the brand, positioning, logo, mark, visual identity, story, and soul of what would become my business—my baby. But because I didn't have any money, I learned to dig inside myself to find what I wanted to say in a logo, in a brand. What did I want to see? I was going to look at it all day long, so what inspired me? I wanted the logo to chant India without people even knowing why. I wanted the logo to be beautiful, something I would want to wear on a shirt. What colors did I like?

The Nike name came from Phil Knight's travels in Greece and the iconic swoosh from a woman designer playing around with strokes for the logo that ended up to be timeless. Starbucks had the mermaid goddess. There was the apple in Apple and the blue bird in Twitter. These are logos that everyone knows, even if the name does not appear. This was the type of logo I wanted.

Armed with another Mason jar filled with warm chai, I went into a local printing and design shop that advertised having a graphic designer on staff and asked for some help. I met Terry, who wore a Phish shirt and sat behind a huge computer monitor with miniature toys around his desk. I immediately knew we would be kindred spirits.

I had two things I wanted to include in the logo: a pillow

with a thread design I liked and a piece of silk fabric I wore in India with a cool pattern. I showed him both pieces of fabric to combine into a photo and a digital logo file. After he took photos and showed me how they could work with the colors I wanted—orange, blue, and red—it was exactly as I hoped and the beginning of many variations that could be called mandala-like.

"What is this fabric from?" Terry asked. It was ripped so it just looked like maybe the top of a tank top.

"A piece of lingerie I bought in India," I said with a smirk. I wanted to bust out laughing and tell him about the first time I wore it, but I couldn't.

I wore it in India with Sri Hari as I tried to distract him from being a celibate monk. While I knew he wasn't a virgin and had past girlfriends, he was also trying to be good with his spiritual habits and hadn't had sex in a while. But our passion and chemistry were well matched, and it was clear we would be having sex soon, so I bought an Indian printed silk negligée. It fit perfectly, but it didn't stay on very long. After I felt the trigger of climax, I sensed Sri Hari stiffen and then heard his heavy breath moan, "Oh Krishna, oh Krishna." *WHAT?* I wanted to scream. But I gulped down my laughter and screamed inside with the cosmic comedy. I couldn't wait to tell my friends! I had never thought before how silly my panting sounded when I occasionally uttered, "Oh God," but in that moment I saw the universal farce of religious affiliations. Do atheists also moan a deity's name under the sheets? There must be some evolutionary psychologist that has looked into this. So interesting!

So no, I didn't mention this to Terry. We weren't *that* kind of kindred spirits, just yet.

But underneath that colorful mandala is the soul of the brand, the name. What does it stand for? What is the mission? What is the purpose other than making money? This tea was going to be my canvas for messaging something larger than just consuming chai. Something I could stand for and something that would inspire me. A word that meant something to me that I could build a brand around.

Creating a recipe from all the chai I had experienced during my three-month trip to India was my escape, so I went back to India for inspiration. And there it was flashing before me in my journal: *bhakti*. In Sanskrit, *bhakti* means "devotion," and it's what brought me to India in the first place.

CHAPTER 4

WORK AS WORSHIP

Mumbai, India, 2002

"Whatever lifts the corners of your mouth—trust that."

—RUMI

I t was my first day in Mumbai without my Hare Krishna chaperone Sri Hari. It felt exhilarating to be alone as I started to explore the city and start my reason for being there: Swadhyay. I walked through the busy humid streets looking for an internet café[12] to notify the Swadhyay offices I was in town and ready to meet.

Mumbai was nothing like I expected. The streets were lined with huge trees, a canopy of green above me. Giant banyan trees burst out of the ground and dripped from the sky, flanked by tall palm trees swaying in the breeze from the Arabian Sea. Long stretches of sandy beaches where teenagers stood in clumps and

---

12 Kids, in the olden days, we had to go to internet cafés and rent computers by the minute to send emails or to go on the World Wide Web. This was before people had personal laptop computers or phones with email, Internet Explorer, or WhatsApp to communicate.

kids flew kites. It reminded me of Southern California. I wasn't expecting to fall in love with the natural beauty of Mumbai. But it was gorgeous. I finally found an internet café and sent them an email and called. That day, I spoke to a man who said to call back the next day.

The next day I called, and again received a cryptic response. The emails went unanswered that I had sent earlier that week. The next day another "Not today, ma'am. Try to call tomorrow" response. And when I asked if I could come by the office and wait, I heard, "No, ma'am. Call tomorrow at ten a.m. Goodbye." Was this entire project and reason for being in India about to fall apart?

I hadn't really grasped "India time" yet and kept feeling defeated and like a failure. Doubt set in. Why didn't they want to talk to me? What was I thinking, that I could just come here and dive into a movement I heard about on NPR?

Then, I saw a shining light walk toward me in the middle of a residential street in Mumbai. A little boy with a wide white smile ran toward me and held onto my hand. I swung him around in circles like a nephew I hadn't seen in months. It was like we were having a reunion, but I'd never met him before. He was wearing a ripped shirt, and his thick hair stood almost in a cresting wave of dirt above his head. In perfect English, he asked, "Can I walk with you?" I responded with a slight head wobble. It was just coming naturally. So much of the head wobble occurs in conversations and so much can be said without words with the right amount of movement to your neck.

As we walked, he picked up and dusted off a mammoth soiled leaf with his shirt until a polished red sheen appeared. He then handed me the leaf as a present. His name was Raju, and he was eight years old. Over the week as I waited to confirm my appointment, he became my new friend and showed me around.

I learned Raju was from a village three hours south of Mumbai.

After his parents died, he rode the train with a brother where he was told he could find a job and food. Raju slept every night around the Gate of Entry, a yellow basalt archway constructed for the arrival of King George and was also where the British pulled away on their last ships after independence in 1948. During the day it's filled with tourists, ice cream vendors, jewelry sellers, and men waving maps or laminated pictures of the nearby Elephanta Island selling ferry tickets. But at night, blankets stashed and tucked in bushes during the day are pulled out, and hundreds of people like Raju sprawl together on the cool cement and sleep under the arch. In the day, most of the families split up to beg. Raju never asked me for money. One night, I found him sleeping outside my guesthouse (his flip-flops under his head as a pillow), and I brought him one of my pillows, one of my shirts, and a blanket. Still, every time I saw him, his big brown eyes rippled joy, even though small crunches were sometimes lodged in the corners of his eyes in the morning from rarely getting a shower.

This was heartbreaking. I sometimes just couldn't handle India. And then this: One day when we were walking around, I asked Raju if he was happy, and he responded with one of his bright smiles. "Of course. Last month a wedding pulled me into their parade," he said, unable to conceal his joy. "And yesterday morning, I was allowed to ride some of the rental bikes for free at 6:00 a.m. because I helped the shop owner clean them. I'm starting to get really good on the bike!"

Wow. This freedom. This living in the moment. This little boy wasn't complaining or judging himself against those kids that get to go to school, that have beds and food, showers and parents. He was finding joy in the little moments. We stopped and I bought Raju a snack. We stood over a big wok of boiling oil and watched samosas flip and spin before being pulled out and placed on newspapers to drain some of the oil. We devoured a plate of samosas with mint and coriander chutney and sipped chai together. Later that day, they confirmed a meeting time to visit the Swadhyay offices and interview the founder's daughter, Jayshree, also known as DidiJi, which means "elder sister" in Hindi. She would also connect me with contacts in some of the villages where I was to travel next.

The next morning, I boarded a bus with other commuters for my first Swadhyay meeting. My head jerked as the bus maneuvered through traffic—huffing and inhaling as it tried to find freedom from Mumbai's congested streets. We passed through a shantytown, where collapsing sheds flapped like faded, frayed Tibetan prayer flags strung along the road. Five million people live just above the curb of homelessness in Mumbai. Throughout India, the number soars to sixty-four million people living in shantytowns.

I tuned in to what was happening with all the people on the streets of Mumbai. Not the sidewalks but the actual roads. Like my favorite Richard Scarry book as a first grader, *Busy, Busy Town*, Mumbai was teeming with people at work. Boys peddled bikes with towering sugarcane branches balanced on their heads. Men with crisp white milkman hats wove through traffic on their bikes balancing tiers of tiffins (silver lunchboxes holding two or three different food compartments). I learned they were dabbawallahs ("one who carries the box"), and they rode their bikes throughout the city, delivering homemade lunches. Not food ordered from restaurants, but prepared at home and then later delivered to workers at lunch. This tradition is over 125 years old. It seemed implausible this could ever work—hot home-cooked lunches delivered daily to work, with people working multiple train and bus routes away? I couldn't wrap my Western mind around it. Why didn't people just bring their lunch to work? Harvard conducted a study and found that there are over four thousand dabbawallahs in Mumbai that successfully deliver two hundred thousand meals a day. Many of them worship and honor the Hindu god Vitthala, who teaches that giving food is a great virtue and one of the best ways to serve. Mothers know this already. As I spent more and more time in India, I realized it's about job creation. Yes, people could bring their lunch to work, but then an entire industry would vanish.

Men carrying cement in wheelbarrows walked right under my window on the bus, maneuvering through traffic. Cows sauntered by in the streets as motorcycles whizzed around them. It all seemed like madness, but no one got hit, and no one yelled at the bike or wheelbarrow or the moped carrying four kids on the back. I couldn't believe what I saw next.

Then, right in the middle of the road, surrounded by men doing road work, there was a vast hole spewing water like a fountain. It was clear water and a woman squatted there, washing her family's clothes with soap. Her toddler, running around her in the middle of the road, was playing in the tiny geyser. I was in shock that no one was honking at this. They honk about everything. No long sighs of disgust or roaring anger out the window to "move out of the road, crazy woman," with a middle finger. No road rage or brandishing guns. Nope. The taxis and buses, cars and cows, mopeds, bikes, wheelbarrows, pedestrians, dabbawallahs, and fruit carts pulled by donkeys all just moved around her like it was an everyday occurrence. I thought, *There is the real sense of compassion, patience, acceptance, and calm in the middle of Busy, Busy Town—in the middle of Mumbai.*

And then I was in love with India again.

After two hours in traffic to get across town—a people-watching extravaganza—I arrived at the Swadhyay offices. I was offered chai when I walked in, and before I could sit down, a steaming cup was placed in my hands. Masala chai. It had more of a bite than I was used to. Not as sweet. Something in my throat began to hum. It was ginger, and it was clove. The cup was too small. It was almost gone, and I wanted more. In India, they drink chai in tiny cups. Little sips throughout the day, not the grande- or venti-sized cups I was used to in America. It wasn't as if I gulped it in one swig, but the man in the office quickly noticed my empty cup and offered me another as I was escorted into Didi's office.

Didi wore a bright peach sari and was perched behind a dark mahogany desk. She was welcoming and warm. "Bhakti is at the center of everything we believe," she said, folding her hands on her desk. "*Bhakti* is derived from the Sanskrit root word *bhaja*, which means to utter, adore, and love. Bhakti devotion has always been considered in the Vedic culture to be in temples, prayers, Brahmans, and songs. It has always been more an individual act or offering to a god. But through the bhakti movement,[13] it was taken out of privacy and into the community. We now use *bhakti* to mean service."

Swadhyay isn't a creed, religion, or NGO. It's a way of life. The movement emphasizes devotional service and an interconnected world family. The first principle of Swadhyay is self-study. This is to withdraw from the extrovert mind and into the introvert mind of examining ourselves. This is a directive toward meditation, solitude, communion with God, gratitude, or centering prayer.

---

13   According to the Vedas (the book of knowledge and the most ancient religious text on Hinduism and Hindu literature compiled from 1200–200 BCE), bhakti is a form of devotion. The bhakti movement arose from the disparity Hindus felt within their religion by the Brahmans or priests who led corrupt lives and the harsh caste system segregating and punishing lower castes. The bhakti movement responded to the egalitarian messages of Islam being spread in India around the unity of God in the thirteenth century AD. Muslims were the ruling class at that time in India. They were converting Hindus with the teachings of universal brotherhood, equality of all in society, the absence of any caste system or untouchables, and the practice of monotheism or oneness of God. Among all these, equality of all men greatly appealed to Hindus. The bhakti movement then aimed to purify the Hindu religion and liberate its people from the priestly class's injustices. It was similar to Martin Luther's thesis on the abuses of the Catholic priests, particularly how they asked for money or "indulgences" to forgive sins and guarantee admission to heaven.

Then, moving into service and treating all people as if they were God. The concept of an indwelling god and giving one's time and expertise as a form of devotion is essential to the Swadhyay philosophy. If God resides in me, then God must reside in others, and therefore we are brethren. Wouldn't we do whatever we could to help or protect our sisters and brothers? The Swadhyay movement aims to create an entirely new type of community.

As she continued to speak, it hit me that I had been searching for a sense of family my whole life, and now I was joining a movement based on universal family. DidiJi continued, "We believe in the acceptance of all religious traditions as a way toward peace. The Swadhyay approach is not just acts of social reform but also acts of showing gratefulness. We can move to a coalition of the world's religions to ensure violence never again, terrorism never again, war never again."

This is what excites me. This hopeful stance that we really can live in a world without terrorism and war that are ultimately all traced back to religious feuds, resources, or land feuds.

DadaJi was a scholar and studied the Bhagavad Gita, philosophy, world religions, and the Vedas since childhood. From this education, he came up with the principles of social experiments and devotional visits. He studied communal farming after he visited a kibbutz in Israel. Volunteerism emerged in villages as a way to show devotion to God. From collective farming, community boats, healthcare, and general stores, these all aligned for a way to create a more peaceful world.

"Forty-five years ago, my father led a group of people for the first *bhakti pheris*, or devotional visits. It was the beginning of his idea around devotional family and a way to transform society through bhakti in action."

She then escorted me to meet her father, who was frail. He had big gold glasses that took up half his face, and his eyes were warm and tender. He touched my hands gently and brought them into his hands.

"There were many skeptics when I founded Swadhyay forty years ago. They said to me, 'How can you succeed without any financial support? Shouldn't you figure out a way to support this idea with capital?' But I told them that if God doesn't want Swadhyay to succeed, then it would not flourish—but if God guides this work, then it will change people's lives."

There are over twenty million people practicing Swadhyay today.

"Thank you for wanting to learn about Swadhyay," he said, leaning toward me. "It's my life's work[14]—it's my bhakti."

That word. That devotion. There it was on his lips, and I wanted to say it out loud. If only I had an inkling at that moment that bhakti would be my life's work too—both with my children and my company. That a little of my faith in humanity had awakened through him, through the Hare Krishnas, and through my time in India.

His teachings were everything I had wanted to learn in grad school or church—or in life—but hadn't yet. Just like the work of A.C. Bhaktivedanta Swami, this wasn't about proselyting or convincing—the hearts opened all on their own through the songs or the service these men inspired. There was no hard sell.

Later that day, I found Raju to say goodbye and give him a pouch of rupees. We shared a Vada burger, a Mumbai specialty.

---

14   Despite the low national and international profile of the Swadhyay movement, DadaJi was recognized by the United Nations for creating innovative sociological models for change and awarded the Templeton Prize for advancing the world's understanding of religion. He was an activist, philosopher, spiritual leader, social revolutionary, and religious reformist. He believes in the acceptance of all religious traditions as a way toward peace. The Pope in her postured, beautiful voice. "Not only am I divine in essence, but also everyone else is equally divine. The Swadhyay approach is not just acts of social reform but also acts of showing gratefulness." She paused, allowing her heavy words to splash around inside of us, and then she concluded with, "We can move to a coalition of the world's religions to safeguard a shared future blessed by God. Swadhyay proclaims a way of service to ensure violence never again, terrorism never again, war never again… and may all the religions proclaim and show in action—forgiveness, life, and love."

It's a thick fried potato (like a hash brown) with American cheese, lettuce, tomato, and a special sauce or chutney on a squishy bun. That day the sauce made me overheat, an obvious damp and red face from the chili heat, but so worth the burn. I felt so full inside, so much love for Mumbai and Raju. He was wearing the blue shirt I had given him with Brooklyn script in orange across the front. It fell off his body, but he still tucked it into his pants and wore it proudly. Excitedly, he said, "It has your name on it! I'll always remember you."

MY DEVOTIONAL VISITS

The next day, I embarked on my bhakti pheris to Daman, Gujarat, to see in action the social experiments transforming the lives of Swadhyay villages. Gujarat is a state on the western coast of India and is Mahatma Gandhi's birthplace. Unlike the Mormon-prescribed proselyting two-year mission work, when one goes for a bhakti pheris, they should not have expectations around the type of response they will receive, nor should they ask for anything. This is about connecting, not converting. Many Swadhyay practitioners devote half of their yearly vacations to go on these devotional visits.

I met my translator Haresh and we drove fast in his white ambassador car, the iconic car of India, as he talked excitedly, telling me his life story. We were heading to the fishing village of Kalai, where he had grown up. He worked for Chevron and was sometimes gone on an oil tanker in the Arabian Sea for months, but practicing Swadhyay was his real passion. We whizzed by Catholic churches[15] and flew down back country dirt roads. "We're here," he said enthusiastically.

---

15   The Portuguese departed Daman in 1962, but only after India took military action in 1961 to take back this enclave and the Portuguese enclave, Goa. Their presence was still coated across stucco buildings in an eggshell blue paint, beautiful bright white and yellow Catholic churches, and gorgeous Portuguese homes in all shades of color.

As I stepped out of the car, crowds of smiling faces came near and encircled us. Everyone was beaming at us as if they were expecting us. I wondered if there was a mistake. Was I intruding on a ceremony? Were they all assembled here waiting for me? Why was everyone smiling at me? I was not prepared for such a greeting. My face was heating up like I had just downed three margaritas.

Haresh promptly guided me to a freestanding wall-less temple, clustered next to homes with wide-mouth porches and a few dangling trees rustling in the breeze from the nearby Arabian Sea. After standing greetings of namaste, with our stretched smiles and prayerful hands either positioned close to our hearts or held above my head, we all walked into the temple and sat down. All the women sat on the floor; saris scattered on the right side of the temple. The men sat down on the left side of the temple. Haresh escorted me toward the front, where we also sat on the floor. Behind us, an altar exhibited a framed color photo of DadaJi and a television screen where they watched weekly lectures from DadaJi.

I thought, *Do I have enough questions?* I felt a little nervous because they were all looking at me to start. I grabbed my notebook and started with thanking them for hosting me and showing me their Swadhyay-infused lives.

There was Anika, a beautiful young woman holding a sleeping baby in the folds of her fuchsia sari, the baby's face glistening with sweaty dew. She said she remembered growing up with much fighting between men. "It seemed like there were always men drinking and fighting. It was scary, and we didn't feel like we could go outside at night. Now, all these men in my community are helping each other. Muslim, Hindu, and Christian—all are coming together without judgment." And then she became a little more animated, her gold earrings dangling with her moving head. "It was always men who spent time in meditation, with gurus, in temples, or studying sacred texts. I wasn't even allowed to touch the Bhagavad Gita because I wasn't considered holy enough. Women were excluded from religious ceremonies for thousands of years, but now we are leading ceremonies and studying spiritual texts with a group of women or *cadera*." A *cadera* is what we would call a woman's group in Boulder—just minus the wine.

There was Manju, who gave up alcohol when his wife started attending Swadhyay lectures and convinced him to join. "Instead of spending every night looking for a drink, I watched DadaJi lecture and realized God was within me. Why would I want to poison my body if God dwells there?"

I couldn't help but wonder if I would be willing to give up alcohol for nightly DadaJi lectures. I wanted it both ways. I wanted to help change the world, but also keep all my Western happy hour comforts.

There was Boli, a stout and sturdy woman in her sixties. She and her husband first saw DadaJi in 1987 and were immediately pulled into his simple message. "It wasn't just Hindu mythology or asking for money, but he was saying the words from his own heart, and we could feel it. We wanted to be a part of something that was love in action."

Testimonial after testimonial, and I was starting to get a contact high. Each one, an aperture into troubled, stifled, or oppressed lives and then transformed by the hope and peace of Swadhyay.

The following morning, I awoke early to go to the *Mastaganda* when the water was calm. This was the community fishing boat that I had heard about in that NPR story. As the morning sun sliced through the hovering blackberry haze, a group of five men hoisted fishing nets and prepared the boat. Slivers of light pranced on their faces. These five men awoke early not to accumulate wealth or swaddle themselves in materialism, but to volunteer.

Their catch was sold in the market, and the proceeds were distributed to those in need.

The magenta flag emblazoned with "Don't Be Careless" rippled and frayed in the wind above the *Mastaganda* as we pulled out of the bay and glided on the Arabian Sea. It smelled of brine. I asked the men how they became involved with Swadhyay and why they donated their time twice a month. A silver-fox man said it best: "No one owns the fish. No one owns wood to make a boat. We are here on earth to serve, to love, to help, and this is just a small way I can show God I'm devoted to his family by volunteering two days a month on this boat."

I wondered, could this work in the US? Could we have some sort of social experiment and contract that everyone devoted just one day every month to help the poor, sick, infirm, and homeless? Even with all our volunteer programs, governmental programs, charities, churches, and NGOs, we still seemed unable to solve homelessness, poverty, healthcare, and child hunger, but maybe we could with more Americans participating in a monthly program like this.

The next day, after I finished my liquid breakfast of two plain *lassis* and four cups of chai, I took an autorickshaw to an internet café. I loved those doorless, windowless, and seatbelt-less rickshaw rides through India. The breeze cooling you off as you zip through traffic. The sometimes-heavy diesel smell one minute and then a cloud of incense the next, or the smell of sizzling fried *chaat* ("snacks") on the streets. I was so far from the States, and I loved it.

In addition to communicating with the people I was supposed to spend the day with in a neighboring Swadhyay village, I wanted to see if Sri Hari had sent more love letters. This was long before the immediate gratification of communicating on WhatsApp. Waiting for an internet connection, I had to endure the little rainbow disk swirling for five minutes, filling me with further anticipation. This was dial-up time, the long beeps and a scratchy sound before the crystal-clear AOL ding of "You've got mail." While I waited, I ordered chai. My constant companion on this India journey. I didn't realize it then, but I was on a tasting tour of chai.

So much waiting in India. Waiting in queues. Waiting for meetings to be finalized. Waiting for six men behind a counter (any counter) to discuss among themselves if they can answer your question or sell you something. Waiting for the emails to load, waiting for a computer, waiting for the electricity to come back on. Waiting for the boy running the internet café to reboot the system or turn on a generator. Wait. Wait. Wait. But I had nowhere to go. I didn't have pressures from work or family; I could sit and wait and mull over everything I had experienced that day until the ding. And there it was, a quick dopamine hit as I saw his name in my inbox. Bing! Another love letter was waiting for me to unwrap. I realized he was just as committed to finding a workstation and writing to me daily as I was to him, telling him about my day and thinking of him. I tried to write all the conversations from the day, all the physical feelings, emotions, and dialogue, but sometimes it just started with, *Can't wait to see you!* Our friendship was deepening, and our flirting permeated every email. I could feel it brewing and was looking forward to kissing Sri Hari again.

Later that day, I met Haresh to drive to a collective farm. Collective farming is prevalent around Gujarat because of the rich soil. We stopped along the road and walked through a sugar-cane field, the tall grass swaying in the breeze. A group of twenty people waited and put out blankets for us to sit on. I couldn't believe more people had come to meet me. I felt bad to take up their time for my silly questions, but they seemed happy to be there. They first served chai. On a silver tray! In the middle of a field. It was so good.

A tall Indian man with white hair explained how they all managed the land together. The tilling was their prayer, the equipment their donation, the watering and harvesting, all their bhakti. The sugarcane was then sold in the markets and given to needy families. On some of the fruit and vegetable plots, the harvest was given directly to families. "We see this as a blessing from God rather than charity. We all love the land."

After our time in the sugarcane field and a tour around the field, we went to the white-haired man's house near the field, where we shared lunch. As soon as I sat on the cement porch, I was served yet another scalding chai. A thin piece of boiled milk skin covered the top, as it was just pulled from the fire. Even in the heat, this hot tea was so good and healing. There is a Hindu belief that guests should be treated as gods, and I felt that everywhere I went.

The women disappeared into the kitchen. I followed and watched them roll dough into balls and smash the balls into their palms—perfect salad-plate-size disks ready for the hot oven to bake into chapati bread. I wanted to talk to these women, but Haresh was in the front of the house talking, so I gestured to ask if I could help roll and smash the dough balls. They immediately knew what I meant and brought me to wash my hands and set a place for me in their circle, where they showed me how to pat, roll, pull, and smack the dough. They couldn't stop smiling, and I couldn't either. I was feeling the power of devotional visits already.

After the somewhat silent but soulful dough circle, we then all sat on the floor and had lunch. The chapati, still warm and malleable, melted in my mouth. It was rubbed with ghee and smelled of fire. With it, we had *chana masala*, or chickpeas in a cumin-garlic-mustard seed curry, that I inhaled and was quickly offered more. I always felt like a greedy eater in India. I couldn't help it; the food was so good, and I seemed hungry all the time.

Plus, it did make the hosts feel good that I was devouring their home-cooked meals.

I didn't see a lot of hugging in India. I did see lots of holding hands. Particularly men holding hands with other men. It was sweet to see boys arm in arm walking down the street or teenage boys holding hands on the street—out of friendship, not romantic. But as we left, I couldn't help but embrace some of my hosts and Haresh. I was just bursting inside with so much appreciation and love. I wanted to squeeze them all. Swadhyay is a revolution in how we relate. If only we could replicate this. All the faith communities around the world joining forces for humanity to show we are one family tree who treat each other as sisters and brothers.

CHAPTER 5

HOW I BUILT THIS

Boulder, Colorado, 2006–2008

"Focusing your life solely on making a buck shows a certain poverty of ambition. It asks too little of yourself. Because it's only when you hitch your wagon to something larger than yourself that you realize your true potential."

—BARACK OBAMA

Bhakti Chai. I had been gestating that name and business for years without even knowing it. It must have settled somewhere in my subconscious while sitting on the floating temple in the Arabian Sea as the fishermen demonstrated their bhakti, or sitting on cramped cement porches surrounded by local villagers watching my every movement as I sipped the boiled chai they had just served me, or with the Hare Krishnas dancing in kirtan—their bhakti through song.

With the basic framework of my company established, the recipe, sourcing, pricing, customers, name, and logo, it was now time to build a company worthy of that name. From the first bhakti traditions nine hundred years ago to the teachings of A.C.

Bhaktivedanta and DadaJi, I wanted to construct the DNA of Bhakti steeped in social justice, feminism, family, and sustainability. It would have to be a different kind of business.

But before I could use tea as my canvas for promoting Bhakti, I needed to build an actual business through sales. I learned early how good closing a deal felt. It's a strong hit of dopamine when making a sale brings you something you want.

In third grade, we all received manila folders with brochures and order forms for a school fundraiser to sell calendars with cats, toffee, or mugs that read "World's Best Mom" with a rainbow. With all the paperwork was a page outlining the prize brackets. Playing cards, board games, Baskin Robbins free cone coupons, some necklaces, and then the grand prizes: a Merlin electric toy that you could play tick tack toe or memory on and that looked like a thick red cell phone from the eighties, and an AM/FM clock radio. I wanted all the prizes, so I set out and went door to door. There were the doors that never opened or closed quickly. Or the bitter grandmas who never ordered and were frustrated you interrupted their afternoon soap operas (I also learned about targeted audiences that year too). But nothing was better than hearing a woman rip the check from her checkbook—the sound of victory. Many nights, it was already dark when I'd come home after selling door-to-door, my hands still cold from biking without gloves when I sat in the warm womb of our kitchen that smelled of sloppy joes while I added up my new orders. At school, I saw my name climb higher and higher on the fundraiser thermometer in the number one slot. I got the Merlin *and* the AM/FM clock radio. Christmas came early that year, and I did it all by myself.

In the first few years of the company, I was the only one to sell my tea. I brought samples to every café in Boulder and tried to convince them to give a small-batch, fresh ginger chai company a chance. Most days, I heard "No." Some café owners gave me the stink eye for even proposing they look at another chai or snubbed me because they were friends with the dudes at another local chai company. And some cafés couldn't care less that their chai was made of fake flavors, syrups, and pumped with preservatives and powders, despite the fact that they promoted and served single-origin organic and fair-trade bougie coffee. But my test market café, Burnt Toast, was flying through chai, and I knew that soon the other cafés would fall and convert.

My inner salesperson was rewarded with the same "close a deal" rush I'd feel many more times. Two accounts became ten and then twenty.

With yet another Mason jar of warm chai, I meet with the owner of a commercial kitchen space, hoping she would rent to me and I could take my brewing out of my kitchen. I walked into the bakery and was smacked with the buttery smell of croissants as if I was in France. A thin woman in her thirties with her hair pulled back by a headband, Shamane whizzed around her kitchen space, pointing out what I could use and what was off-limits. The kitchen was crammed with quiche in cooling racks, industrial Hobart mixers, fondant for wedding cakes, a wall of flour and sugar bags packed high, stainless-steel tables, two huge stoves, and the three-sink sanitizing station.

I toured my new office with wonder—a colossal walk-in cooler for all my gallons of chai to store in between deliveries. The two large gas stoves could fit five of my twenty-gallon pots. That meant I could make one hundred gallons in one night. While she showed me around, her assistant was brushing an egg wash over croissant dough, smearing it all over those tender belly folds. I was salivating and beaming at the same time. It felt so exciting to make my little chai recipe surrounded by all these shiny pieces of equipment and mouth-watering baked goods. And to share the space with other food and beverage entrepreneurs.

I felt giddy to be moving into this next step of a business. Soon, my twenty accounts turned into thirty. One night a week brewing turned into two nights a week as I secured more café accounts. I worked my day job (as a full-time development director for the same reproductive justice organization that loudly announced I was carrying twins) until 5:00 p.m. every day. Then some weeknights or on the weekends, I brewed tea, pressed ginger, ordered ingredients, created invoices, delivered chai, and did everything else it took to build a company by myself.

I would often pick up my kids from daycare at 5:00 p.m. and then deliver chai. I remember one time running into a café and dropping off six gallons. I waited for the manager to sign the invoice and write me a check. It was likely eight minutes. When I came outside, there were two cop cars. Apparently, some Karen called the cops. I was livid. "Who called the police?" I demanded to know, looking around and staring down people in the parking lot. The car was locked, with the windows halfway down and the kids safely buckled in their car seats. Kids can't sit and stare out a window anymore? They have to be chaperoned, and scheduled by helicopter parents, and fed a snack every fucking thirty minutes? No. Not my kids. They sometimes need to sit and look out the window with boredom while their mother multitasks and brings in money for dinner.

The police said someone called, worried that the kids could be stolen.

"Who is going to kidnap twins?" I said. "That's ridiculous. And good luck to them! Kidnappers couldn't handle these two."

In Boulder there isn't that much going on, so they rushed to the scene of two towheads in car seats looking out the window. Here I am trying to build a business while I parent and work full time, and someone is afraid of a kidnapper. Karens need to find other hobbies than involving themselves in the lives of strangers. The cops sided with me and just said to not leave them in the car again. *Oh okay, Officer, I'll never run into a store again without dragging two kids inside with me*, I thought to myself. But I said, "Yes, sir," and drove away.

MISSION IN A BOTTLE

With the shell of the company established and customers happy with my weekly deliveries, it was time to focus on the DNA of the business. Even the word *business* conjured up for me boring cubicles, stale suits, sexism, rules, male privilege, misogyny, a rigged system, and greed. There seemed to be something soulless about business. It always seemed to make the wealthy wealthier on the backs of someone else.

Yvon Chouinard,[16] the founder of Patagonia, wrote in *Let My People Go Surfing*, "I've been a businessman for almost fifty years, and it's still difficult for me to say those words, as is it for someone to admit being an alcoholic or a lawyer. I've never respected the profession. It's business that has to take the majority of the blame for being an enemy of nature, destroying native cultures, taking from the poor and giving to the rich, and poisoning the earth with the effluent from its factories."

I didn't have a positive paradigm about business either. I grew up in the eighties, when "Shop till you drop" was the mantra, and people even wore that phrase proudly, sometimes bedazzled on bulky sweatshirts. Consumerism was pumped into our veins like a drug, and I hated all the waste and greed it created.

The more you buy, the happier you are, they told us. But I didn't know then it was the shareholders who were the happy

---

16 He not only built an activist company funding global environmental projects and legislation with $10 million a year, but he also created products using materials less harmful to the environment, and became a certified B Corp. He recently sold the entire company to make the earth their only shareholder. The company's purpose is not to grow to extract wealth for stakeholders. It's mission is to save the planet.

ones—stockpiling billions on the backs of workers paid below minimum wage or children in China or Vietnam sewing our clothes. Shopping became a hobby, consumerism a religion. Americans, for the first time in history, went into serious debt because of shopping. I hated learning that since 1978, CEO compensations rose 1,000 percent, compared to 11 percent for the average worker. I hated that unions were becoming impotent, and the earth was being pillaged for profits.

So it was only natural that when I built a company, I would rebel against the status quo of what I knew about business. Try to pry open some of the nonprofit principles I'd learned in school and then later reinformed studying Hare Krishna and Swadhyay. I was inspired by companies like Patagonia, Ben and Jerry's, the female-founded Body Shop, and Newman's Own—companies with a conscience. I wanted it to be a for-profit company modeled after the values of nonprofits and social justice organizations. Could I create a business that felt more like a movement that helped and didn't harm? And also strive for what Aristotle called "human flourishing," or a purpose beyond the material?

Aside from the dark inequities, lack of regulation, climate damage, corporate lobbyists, sexual harassment, underpaying women, and greed of capitalism, on the positive side it has been responsible for unprecedented advancements in the world. Two hundred years ago, 85 percent of the world's population lived in extreme poverty; today, it is 16 percent. Life expectancy increased, and malnourishment dropped 50 percent. The economist Deirdre McCloskey argues the most important factors in free-enterprise capitalism are the entrepreneur and innovation, combined with freedom and dignity.

There is a new type of corporation that wants to do good in the world. They are called B Corps, or benefit corporations, and they are shifting the way we look at corporations. This is not the buy one, give one away marketing tool like TOMS shoes or other granola bar companies. This is how one structures their entire organization from the ground up with the highest standard of verified social and environmental performance with transparency, to balance purpose with profit. They are trying to build a movement of like-minded businesses but also infiltrate business schools to teach business with a new paradigm of considering the stakeholders as not just investors, but like Yvon Chouinard has demonstrated, the earth, employees, and the community as major stakeholders. I wanted to be a small part of this unique category of capitalism that created societal and environmental transformation in addition to economic growth and freedom. Bhakti became one of the first certified B Corps in Colorado. There are now 2,500 B Corps in more than fifty countries.

The giving ethos of Bhakti started with monthly tithing. In Hinduism, *Seva* is the concept of service and in Buddhism, *Dana* is the practice of giving and the virtue of generosity. I watched my grandparents hand over an envelope for the offering plate every Sunday, and they taught me early the importance of tithing. But I wanted to support something other than building a bigger church or missionaries proselytizing in Africa. I wanted to fund women, girls, and the environment.

Women and girls are the population most vulnerable, and funding dollars disproportionately go to men globally, while women and girls bear the brunt of poverty, oppression, forced childhood marriage, war, rape, violence, climate change, and inequality. David Wallace Wells describes this as a climate caste system. While the ruling class continues to bicker and, in many cases, even deny the looming planet that is either on fire or underwater, one hundred million people will be dragged into poverty due to climate destruction over the next decade, undeservedly affecting more women and the poor.

I set up monthly automated payments to nonprofits so that it was a part of our operating budget. It was built into the DNA of the business model. Bhakti supported organizations like Planned Parenthood, Global Fund for Women, and the Urgent Action Fund, which works on the ground with activists trying to bring about changes in Iran, Afghanistan, and India. From helping women in Nepal have their voices included in the constitution to working with women in Romania fighting to ratify the prevention and elimination of violence against women.

I was bringing my concoction out in the world, and now I wanted to paint her in gold. Not the gold of men and greed, stealing and wars, but the gold of giving. The gold of goddesses lighting bonfires in celebration. The gold of sunflowers and shimmering aspens in the fall. The gold reflection of early morning light, full of hope. The liquid gold I was making in big batches.

Meanwhile, my twins were entering the terrible twos. Whining honks punctuated every sentence. Physical assaults against each other when my back was turned. With twins, it was like living in the Twilight Zone of double terrible twos, and it was always two against one—me. They were armed with large sticks, spray bottles, and new big teeth for biting each other. At times they seemed to have no consciences, no thoughtfulness, and no awareness, and I feared they could be psychopaths. But then I remembered they didn't have fully formed frontal lobes, so I tried to wrestle back control, love, negotiate, distract, and teach—but I was dismantled many days. They were trying to take me down. But then they rolled over on me and gave me their bellies to tickle like fat cats, and I knew they were going to be alright. They had such joy and bright eyes sometimes, it was contagious. In an instant they would be smiling and laughing again. I fell in love with them more and more each day.

Things were unraveling quickly with Judd. We had been

fighting more about money, household responsibilities, and the inequality in our work/home lives. He wasn't pulling his weight, not as a financial partner nor as a co-parenting household partner. My increased ambition only made him slow down and then fueled his anger and resentment. I couldn't be with someone who flew off the handle so often and made me feel unsafe. I saw a future with him, and it wasn't what I wanted. Always struggling financially, fighting, the fear of that thrown trash can at my windshield again as I backed out of the driveway with my kids in the back seat heading to work and dropping them at daycare—cracking more than just the windshield next time. His flowy spiritual pants and prayer beads strung around his wrist couldn't mitigate his outbursts. I was bruised but not broken, and after I got my brewing out of that A-frame, I worked on getting us out next.

It took over six months to save enough money from my full-time day job to move out and pay monthly rent while keeping my business afloat. But I found the perfect two-bedroom house in Boulder, within walking distance to two parks, and started a new life with Ryzen and Veda. Our bedrooms were connected with a small Jack and Jill bathroom, and most nights, one of them would wander in to sleep with me and our cat. There wasn't a third bedroom for Moe, but I made a little room off the living room his space when he came to stay. I thought of him as my son, too, and wanted him to always know I was one of his moms and to keep the four of us family even though Judd couldn't join. I never signed a marriage certificate, but in Colorado I still had to file for a divorce and sign a divorce decree. So much for my no strings attached plan. Then, Judd tried to sue me for half of Bhakti Chai. A company that wasn't even paying me yet. A company I was self-funding by working a full-time job—and supporting my kids. This didn't exactly make for the most amenable divorce. It added an entirely new level of combative stress to my life. While I had so much anger at Judd for trying to take money from the woman supporting his children, and lost so much respect for him, in the end, the divorce gave me two days a week that he was responsible for the kids, and I could devote that time to building Bhakti.

FAMILY TREE, FAMILY TEAM

One summer night, when I was at Shamane's brewing, I went out back and slumped down on the ground, leaning against the concrete wall that was still warm from cooking in the sun all day. I lit a clove cigarette and exhaled like a cartoon character, stress visibly seen and heard. It was after 2:00 a.m., and because I had to zigzag around town looking for spices when my order didn't show up, I was four hours behind.

These were pause buttons for me to check my sanity. *How many more nights can I do this alone? How am I going to get this to the next level? When can I hire help?* I looked down at my arms. Burns from spattering scalding tea and hot pots sliced across my forearms. I looked like a cutter. I was hitting my wall—against this hot wall—and it was pushing me to change. The crickets were cheering loudly, a concert just for me. Then, a train overpowered that delicate concerto with a boom. It blared its long-approaching echo and kept blasting as it came by on the tracks near the bakery. I was done brewing by myself. I needed out of that hot kitchen.

I kept thinking of Regan. I was still heartbroken by a love of my life plunging into an incurable bipolar depression that I was powerless to help him conquer.

The first day this love, Regan, walked into the café where I was working during grad school, our gaze seemed to stick. I was glued to his sparkling Paul Newman blue eyes as he ordered a cappuccino and a handful of chocolates. I acted nonchalant and uninterested. But he was so tall and handsome. It could have been just another transaction: order, money, steaming milk, pulling espresso, with small talk. But after I made his cappuccino, he threw me one of those round Lindt chocolate balls across the café. A line drive to my right hand…and I caught it. And then he cheered, loudly. He said, "Enjoy." With a little flirty grin "in one bite." I was intrigued.

The chocolate was pure white chocolate and smelled like Easter. Something inside of it whispered this guy was going to be ride—yes, maybe a little Willy Wonka's psychedelic ferry ride, but also a sexy stroll, stopping and kissing every step—because it was just too hard not to touch each other.

Our banter and courtship began quickly. One day he turned his back to put a sugar packet into his cappuccino and there they were—the first beats of real intrigue. Handcuffs were dangling from the back of his jeans, and a gun holster with a gun. *WTF.* My barista friends and I called him "Shooter." When I wasn't working, they called me to say, "Shooter's here. He's asking when you work next? Should I tell him your schedule?" "Of course!" I would reply. I wanted to see him again.

Regan was a federal agent and had just finished law school, bought an Art Deco mansion in Detroit down the street from Aretha Franklin to remodel, and was ten years older than me. We fell crazy in love and were happy—for about a year. But then he became paralyzed with depression or had bouts of agitated mania. I even accompanied him to the fancy treatment center, Sierra Tucson, where we sat starstruck in family groups with Josh Brolin and Barbara Streisand, ate clean food, and hiked around cacti-covered mountains that looked like coral reef. He tried a handful of medications, and soon he was his old handsome smart funny self again, the one I fell in love with. But within nine months, the demons returned.

Regan would know what to do. He would be a sounding board

for me. Maybe he'd even come out and help me build Bhakti. But, he hadn't called me back yet. He was on my mind all week after springing upright in bed a week earlier, clutching my chest. I had a dream he died. The next morning, in my office at work, I dialed his number and leaned back in my swivel chair, smiling while it rang. I couldn't wait to hear his raspy voice and say something sarcastic. He would be so proud of me, calling me a little sassy entrepreneur selling my "granola" drinks, even though he was a granola sometimes too. He'd be floored by how much chai I could make and sell. He'd probably want to invest! I could already hear our conversation, like we'd always done, jumping on our imaginary swing set as we bantered on the phone. We could have sold tickets to all those quick-witted conversations laced with sexual innuendoes. We would crack ourselves up sometimes with long pauses of laughter and then the sound of us lighting our cigarettes.

It had been three years since I called him to say I was pregnant and having a commitment ceremony. He said, "Well, I guess this is it then, goodbye forever." We had always reconnected after years of not talking, so I thought he was just being dramatic. But that dream made me take action to see if he was doing okay. He had changed his phone number, so I called his law office in Michigan. A woman answered and said he wasn't in the office. I left my name and number, but a week later he still hadn't called me back.

For now, I'd have to figure this out all alone.

Even as a radically independent introvert entrepreneur, I needed a community. A family of my own creation—a team and support system. I didn't read team building, hiring, or "how to develop culture" books—I didn't have time. Honestly, with my day job, the twins, driving, and Bhakti, I couldn't have gotten my hands on a book if I'd wanted. So I trusted my gut. It was time to take another leap of faith and jump into hiring people to join me on this crazy ride.

The next layer of scaffolding in constructing my chai empire was building a team, a family. Building a business was like birthing a child, so it was only natural I wanted a family to help with all the feedings. A fun team to make things happen and help push her up the hill.

This was also about creating my own family.

When I was growing up, the idea of a family always felt elusive. I was always looking for my "real" family I didn't know. It was unspoken, but I knew from an early age that I was alone in the world. I sometimes felt like a foreign exchange student visiting for one semester with my grandparents and extended family. During the excruciatingly long prayers at the dinner table, where I would watch every chin tucked to every chest and eyes squinted shut, I would wonder where the trap door was that led to my "real" family.

Although my biological parents were physically absent, they were wildly present in my daydreams and imagination. This is common in grief, a type of denial or magical thinking. I envisioned my mother returning after some international sabbatical and cooking us something spicy and exotic instead of the green bean casserole sprinkled with potato chips that was on my plate. My father would, of course, be the wealthy businessman like Daddy Warbucks pulling up in a limo. But they never showed.

In the first twenty-five years of my life, I was on a scavenger hunt, trying to unearth pieces of my mother. I wanted to understand what happened that first year of my life with her.

The first clue about my mother surfaced when I was in second grade on the morning before a field trip to Canada. My grandmother pulled the terry cloth robe cords tight above her stomach bulge, sectioning off the region that had once incubated six children, the eldest of which was my mother. "I don't even know if it's in here." My grandmother's morning voice quivered with a mild annoyance as she continued to flip through manila folders in the basement filing cabinet. "Why couldn't you have told me about this last night?" Then she gave an extended sigh as she threw each drawer back into the cabinet before opening the next.

I couldn't answer. I couldn't voice my anxiety as my classmates ran into school, waving their birth certificates for our upcoming field trip to Canada, proud and excited to reveal their middle names or birth weights. I couldn't describe to my grandmother the embarrassment I envisioned sitting with my classmates in the back seat of a car at the Ambassador Bridge entrance, hovering over the churning Detroit River and handing over proof to everyone that I didn't really have parents. Confirmation I was an orphan. But my eyes were speaking, probing for signs of my mother in those concealed files.

I stared at my grandmother's face, smooth and plump from her nightly Oil of Olay. After numerous sighs and shuffled papers, she pulled my birth certificate from a folder entitled "Janet." I stared at the word, scratched in slanted pencil strokes, and quickly memorized its place in the sequence of folders for later inspection. She handed me the birth certificate, but not before folding it with two clenched creases. I ran upstairs to wait for my ride, for the first time holding a piece of my mother.

I planned my "Janet" folder invasions for Thursday nights when my grandparents were at choir practice. After the polite goodbyes and the garage door thumped against the pavement, I crept downstairs, the same staircase my mother skipped up as a teenager. I laid the folder in my lap. After scanning stale, abstract legal documents, I discovered a sealed envelope marked with the same pencil scratch as my birth certificate folder. It read, "Found in her pocket."

I slowly tore the envelope, and a sage-green bead the size of a walnut rolled out in my hand. I held it to my nose and inhaled, hoping for olfactory memory. Unfortunately, it was barren of any residual pheromones, just the faint wood stank of an ordinary bead. But there was something about this bead that was once so close to my mother that it could have felt her body stiffen or may have rolled and shifted when her spirit released.

It was in my grandfather's art studio, where he painted in solitude and read the Bible, that I discovered the gold: handwritten letters from my mother.[17] Small cards were constructed out of the inside of cereal boxes and attached with ribbons. Other letters were smudged with crispy leaves and dried flowers. I combed through each pile, scanning for my name and hoping to find the letter she wrote to me explaining it all. I wanted to hear her voice; I wanted to read her words to me about how she died, why, and who my father was.

I scattered the letters and envelopes on my grandfather's horizontal easel, carefully moving his watercolors and brushes with an intruder's attention to detail. Even the envelopes that housed these treasures were dripping with my mother. Watercolor strokes shaped lush mountain scenes marinating in dew; pastels

---

17 Dear Mom, Sittin' in the sun......writin' to my loved ones. I've been reading stories at Sally's daycare and volunteering at the rec center in town and taking yoga at the Y. On our hike this morning, Sue and I found a whole pile of old mason jars just begging to be filled with applebutter. So we lugged them all home and sat in the kitchen chatting while we sugared apples. Okay, Mom find an easy chair, sit yourself down, and...... "get easy." I'm getting a paying job! Now don't pass out—it's true. Now all your worries are over, I'm not going to rot away to nothingness in this cabin. I'm going to strike out into the world of the working people and find my way. They're going to pay me to do massage at the Glenwood Vapor Caves! Everyone there, including the owner, seems like they're really involved in living. The mountain sun and snow are comforting me, but Colorado is getting so touristy, mom. It's so sad to see a good friend go down. People move here everyday—but they don't have love. I guess that's why they come here, thinking they will find love in the mountains. But then they just create their worlds again, condominiums, shopping centers, money money, which then keeps everyone good and busy—and distracted. I guess it's starting to do that all over the world. Mom, what I meant before in my letter is that sharing your real self can be hard, but I love you anyway so let's just try to communicate. So you have a daughter living in a cabin in Colorado, is that so bad? If it is so bad, tell me about it. If you can't share your REAL self...what is sharing all about? Too bad there isn't an island where people could go who wanted to make a life out of love. Starting from scratch with trust, honesty, and true connections. I guess life is supposed to be hard at this point. Otherwise I would never leave home. I'd just get nice and comfortable and stay where I was adjusted. Have kids and not hassle with anything else. But I've seen too much of life to hide from it. It's REAL!!! And you have to stand up for what you've seen and believe. Love, Jan

smoothly blended maroon and rose-rippled sunsets. Colored pencils sketched turquoise and yellow hot air balloons that floated off the page. I felt disappointed that there were no letters written to me, explaining it all. When the streetlight coating poured into the window with a prowler's alarm, I knew my grandparents would be home soon, and I fled.

There were also no pictures of my mother when I was growing up. I remember the hum of the slide projector warming up and making shadow puppets on the screen. Photos of my grandparents on trips, baby photos, aunts and uncles at prom, at camps, weddings, and on car trips. And then, in a click, I spotted my mother. She showed up infrequently—most of the slides had been removed already, but a few were missed. In bell-bottom jeans and a yellow T-shirt, she was beaming, leaning next to an avocado-colored Pinto car. I felt the room sink. It was a reminder that she was gone for them, too, not just for me. I could feel their grief in those beats of silence. These seconds on the screen were treasures for me. But then my grandfather advanced the slide, and she was gone, like a ghost.

My mother left boxes of journals and letters with her friends in Colorado before she died. They kept them for years until I finally tracked them down. This was how I eventually found the name of my biological father. Decades before Ancestery.com, 23andMe, or even Facebook, I had to go old school and use the landline phone. I called a handful of wrong numbers until a woman answered and asked who was calling. *Could this be his wife?* I wondered. *Did she know I existed?* "That's okay. I'll call back," I said. The next time I called, again this woman answered and hesitated upon hearing my voice. She almost pleaded with me to take a message, so I started, "My name is Brook and," she cut me off. "You mean Baby Brook? We have a baby picture of you on our mantel," she squealed. It was shocking to hear I was recognized, and it sounded like acknowledged. But I also thought, *Flaunting my picture but not one phone call? Telling your wife about me, but not attending one soccer game or giving me one birthday gift?*

When I met my biological father at the Denver airport, he was holding a bouquet of red and yellow snapdragons from his garden, and he did apologize for being MIA for twenty years. That was not his wife, but a girlfriend, and he said he was waiting until he had his life together to contact me. I not only made a new family connection with my biological father, who would become a good friend, and who I've now known longer than the twenty years I didn't, but I also gained three younger half-siblings, and one would become integral in building out the family tree of Bhakti.

My first actual employee was my nanny, Morgan—with big sparkling green eyes, wavy brown hair, and a vivacious sense of humor like Carol Burnett mixed with a Lucille Ball daring spirit. Her outgoing energy was infectious. Morgan helped me build Bhakti from the first few months of crusted tea and spices on my stove at home. As I rushed out the door in the morning to my day job (I was always late) and handed her Ryzen and Veda, she offered to scrub the chai film from my previous night of brewing four pots on my stove. She saw the madness of my kitchen brimming with pots, spices strewn on the floor, countertops sticky with spilled sweet tea, and handwritten notes to myself fiddling with the recipe. She was a natural salesperson, who made everyone laugh and feel good about life. Soon she was delivering gallons to cafés for me and would later become our demo coordinator and eventually our director of sales. She helped transform Bhakti into the family and tribe during our peak.

My second employee was a tall, lean, tan woman named Jen. She was looking for work experience in natural foods before she went to school for her MBA. Morgan, the natural connector, introduced us. She started to press ginger, brew tea, clean pots, deliver—basically do whatever Bhakti needed. With just that increased labor, sales began to double as I could focus on selling more.

I needed someone else to help brew with Jen and immediately thought of my new half-brother, who lived in Denver. He had a baby girl and was looking for work. I could only offer him part time at first, but he eventually came on full time and was promoted to master brewer and later brewery manager. This idea of building a family within my business actually had some blood to it. Not knowing him growing up, it was fun to get to know him as a friend and be an older sister for the first time in my life.

Then, there was the sixty-year-old tan and buff Buddhist delivery driver, Dennis. He packed up his refrigerated van with our gallons and delivered them to all the new accounts we were securing in Denver and other cities around Colorado.

A newly graduated CU student reached out and asked to intern for free. Her name was Alessandra, and she had pale strawberry blonde hair and a slight Georgian accent. She proved herself in a month of doing any and everything to help and became my first assistant, then demo coordinator, then sales and marketing officer. I felt bad not paying her much, but she wanted the experience and the freedom to take off for weeks at a time on trips, so it was a win-win.

Startups need to have a thread of family. It was a tapestry weaving in dedication to the larger goal of bringing Bhakti to the masses and doing well while having fun and mutual respect. I couldn't have started Bhakti without the support of so many friends or what they've become—family. But what happened was that friends then became employees. Employees later became friends. Family members became employees. It wasn't until I built my business that I realized I was stitching together what I had always wanted—a rowdy, liberal, free-thinking, partying, smart, kindred-spirit foodie family.

IT'S GETTIN' REAL UP HERE IN THE WHOLE FOODS PARKING LOT

I started meeting strangers in parking lots at night, not for illicit sex but for drug deals. These were wide-eyed Bhakti Chai daily users that instead of buying a cup a day at their favorite café, wanted to buy a gallon directly from me and make it at home. They would do anything for their addiction and met me at odd hours and in random parking lots. Sometimes it was the library or a corner liquor store. I'd show up, throw open my trunk, and be ready for business.

I charged twenty-five dollars a gallon, so pulling in an extra hundred dollars a week was worth it. The calls increased, and soon I was doing weekly "office hours" in the Whole Foods parking lot in Boulder. My kids settled into their car seats and waited with me. They stuffed granola bars into their mouths, sucked on orange sections, and decimated yogurt pouches. Fragments of these reappeared in the crevices of those car seats weeks later.

As the business grew and demands increased, it just became too much orchestration. Too many people wanted me to sell at different times. Waiting and texting with customers "on their way" or hoping that one guy who ordered three gallons but never called me back to confirm would show up—waiting until nine at night would be worth it, but only if he showed. I needed to find an outlet. Somewhere I could send people to buy Bhakti instead of from the trunk of my car. And there it was in gleaming green letters—Whole Foods.

I didn't know there were official intermediaries in the grocery process. Buyers reviewed and decided the fate of your product. Sometimes this was just one person, so you better hope they were having a good day or liked you or knew what chai was. Grocery store buyers receive five hundred new products a month to review, and most are never tasted or even looked at for serious consideration. There are official times buyers look at new products (review calendars) and people who get paid to present to buyers (brokers), bring products to Whole Foods (distributors), decide where products go on the shelf (planogram managers), place the products on the shelf with price tags (merchandisers), analyze products and accept or discard them from reams of data (category analysts), and even those who force you to put your product on sale while they pocket half so the customer only gets a little off the price (retail promotion managers).

But I didn't know of any of this then, so I just waltzed into the store with a Mason jar of chai and asked to speak to a manager. The lady at the information/customer service/returns desk paged someone. Enrique strolled up with gloves on and a vest, having just come from the refrigerated rooms in the back of the store. He was the dairy manager. I gave him the Mason jar and started walking to the place in the store where I thought it would live. I explained how Bhakti was different and Whole Foods didn't have any fresh chai, only the boxed stuff.

"I have a local following from my café business, and I've been selling it to people in parking lots who want it. I need a place to send all my gallon customers who want to make it at home."

"Oh, I've heard of Bhakti; people have asked about it," he said.

I couldn't have asked for a better response. Having a little street cred went a long way. He turned the Mason jar around and around, looking for something. "You'll need a nutritional label on this, as well as a UPC code, and what are you thinking in terms of price?"

I responded, "ten ninety-nine?" It was a concentrate, after all, and that quart would give people six to eight cups of chai. They paid four dollars for one cup of chai at the café. I knew about nutritional labels and had scanned them throughout various health fads, looking for fat, carbs, and sugar, but I didn't know how to get one or a UPC, but I played along and said I'd have it in a week.

"Oh, and we'll send someone out to your facility to do a quality check."

Huh? I thought but didn't give on.

"Oh, sure. How do I schedule that?"

A week later, a woman with a clipboard walked around Shamane's kitchen as I showed her our equipment, processes, and storage. And that's how I was able to get one little shelf space for Bhakti, one little slot to send all my late-night parking-lot devotees. While it was just one store, I now had a new goal: to have Bhakti in every Whole Foods in Colorado and then in the country.

It felt like such big news. Bhakti was really launching! My hard work over the last year was starting to gain traction. The following week I went back into the store, and it was like picture day for my kids when I saw her on the shelf. Next to the kombucha and iced tea but with only one little row, or facing. All neat and organized with a tiny shelf tag. My baby was growing up so fast; I felt so proud. Then, I felt a pang of panic. What if people didn't buy it?

Failure in the food industry is almost inevitable. Over twenty thousand new products hit the shelf every year, and 85 percent of those will fail within eighteen months. And those are the ones that made it to the grocery store to die; thousands never make it on the shelf. Handcrafted, healthy, amazing farmers-market brands or the products spending all their money to formulate and prepare only to be denied at the very end.

A graveyard of businesses, ideas, formulations, money, and products. Where the majority of anything you've ever handled or consumed will eventually end up, save the legacy brands like Coke, Frito Lay, Smucker's, Hormel, and General Mills. I think of all the products I loved and then just never saw again. Those organic ice cream sandwiches tasted better than the strawberry shortcake pops from the ice cream man. Gone. Those sweet potato chips dusted with spice just a few years before the buffalo/Sriracha-on-everything trend. Gone. That iced tea everyone loved called Honest Tea. Gone.

In beverage, those numbers are worse: 90 percent will fail in the first year, and 99 percent will die before reaching $10 million in revenue. Luckily, I didn't know this then, and I followed some imaginary pull that my chai wanted to be out in the world.

Getting that first check from Whole Foods six weeks later was gold. I wanted to frame the check but couldn't afford not to cash it ASAP and shove it into a twenty-four-hour ATM. I can relate to the quote from the founder of Jeni's Ice Cream, "Entrepreneurship isn't just an art, it's a two-way conversation with customers." I was so thankful to those parking-lot customers that forced me to expand into the retail landscape and then to customers that requested unsweetened chai, my second SKU.

Today, you could never stroll into a Whole Foods[18] store with a Mason jar of homemade chai, and get approval. This was back when employees working in the cheese department were basically cheese sommeliers who spent hours researching regions and flavors so they could recommend pairings in their twenty-minute tasting venture with you.

Some will say that Whole Foods didn't let their employees unionize or that John Mackey was a libertarian uninterested in universal healthcare who could have done more before selling out to Amazon. But he did what he could, and I found solidarity in his mission-driven company and inspiration in some of his words: "Business has a fundamental responsibility to create prosperity for society and the world. It's a holy calling. No human creation has had a greater positive impact on more people, more rapidly,

---

18 Whole Foods was decentralized then, and was looking for regional brands, unique products, and local entrepreneurs. They even launched a local producer's loan program, giving small brands $100K in loans to help them get set up and scale for WFM. They encouraged innovation. Now, with the behemoth of Amazon owning it, and pumped full of Walmart, Costco, and Home Depot executives, Whole Foods has become a different entity. Before Amazon took over, activist investors dove in and wrangled Whole Foods from its path of food enlightenment. While he began as an unlikely entrepreneur (no college degree and never having taken a business class), co-founder John Mackey can trace his interest in co-founding WFM from his counterculture time in the seventies practicing yoga, meditation, and becoming a vegetarian and vegan.

than free enterprise capitalism." While this is moving in the right direction, business could be doing more and making more impact.

In *Winners Take All*, Anand Giridharadas argues that it's not actually the white global elite businessmen that can solve today's problems that were created by centuries of their industrialized, free market, greedy, 1 percent capitalist brethren. They have too much to lose if the tables were turned to increase wages, expand unions, or invest in saving the planet. His solution was not that business fix our social and environmental ailments, but in fact, the government already has the taxing arm established that could regulate, create more equality, invest in education, and balance too big to fail corporations that don't pay taxes, and save the planet.

If Whole Foods gave my generation clean, flashy stores that played The Smiths, Stevie Wonder, and Sade while shopping for organic, fair-trade, gourmet, and interesting treats, a stark contrast to the dusty A&P or Kroger stores I had frequented as a child, then Trader Joe's gave us connection. The founder, Joe, peeled back the buying experience and the latent desires of the consumer, linking the act of shopping as an experience. For Joe, it wasn't just about cutting out the middleman for lower prices but curating never-before-seen products and homegrown marketing he created that signified identity: "I wanted to create a silent conspiracy among all the overeducated, underpaid, well-traveled, and inquisitive people that when they moved down the aisles, they would read secret messages on the products and get a chuckle. I wanted to flatter their vocabulary and tickle their minds with inspiration and interesting foods." He saw business and the food industry as a creative act, bringing the surprise delights of travel on the shelf of his stores.

The average person will spend 2 percent of their life in a grocery store. It's probably closer to 4 percent for women, and I've probably spent more like 6 percent adding in all the Bhakti work in a grocery store. I've always loved the smell of natural food co-ops. As soon as I walked through the door that jingled, my Pavlov's dog receptors juiced up. I loved to linger at the bulk bins as a teen-ager. I would buy yogurt-covered pretzels and tofu frozen yogurt. It sounds gross, but they masked any Umami undertones with deep, dark chocolate or bright mint. It was good. They became my comfort places when I moved somewhere. All through college, graduate school, my first real job, and my first apartment, I sought out the closest health food store, never knowing that it would inform my life's path. I joined these co-op markets religiously, knowing I was supporting more than just my favorite brand of organic corn chips or the bulk bins, but a natural food movement.

At this point, though, I still thought items in Whole Foods were curated and put there because they were the best quality or the healthiest—that Whole Foods built those end aisle displays to showcase the highest quality new corn chip or drink. I didn't yet know what Benjamin Lorr in *The Secret Life of Groceries* revealed as the underground stench of big retail grocery chains. They didn't just make profits off the products they sold, but double-dipped and charged brands other mandatory fees[19] to make profits. To be at the end aisle, near the register, on display, or to even to be

---

19 Retailers don't make their profits selling products, but charging vendor fees. Buyers are not foodies looking to give their customers the best possible product or go out on food adventures, sampling at farmers market booths or abroad for the coolest new empanada, dip, sauce, or fermented drink; they have financial bottom lines. They aren't scanning for the cleanest, organic, fair-trade, non-GMO, non-slave labored, woman-owned in 100 percent compostable packaging—nope. They are looking for brands that will slide them money under the table to get them on the shelf and keep sliding them money all year round to stay on that shelf. They have a bottom line on products moving, costing them less, selling them for more, and getting free products to sell at a 100 percent profit. And then, every year, they have to increase profits further to hit more significant goal numbers created by their bosses and overall private equity bosses. One Whole Foods global buyer described it as crack. Every year the machine needed more money, so they asked brands to give them more. With Amazon, brands are forced to provide WFM even more. Each retailer asks for money for those six inches of real estate on the shelf. These payments in 2005 amounted to $76 billion taken by retailers in what's called "advertising" or "marketing fees." But this is not advertising or marketing in the traditional sense of an actual ad or brand recognition. It's just one of the many fees distributors and retailers mandate to do business with them. And you can't say no. I tried many times, resulting in being thrown off the shelf, buyers never returning emails, bills sent for payment that I never agreed to but had to pay. Costco doesn't do this. They make money on their membership fees, so instead of charging the entrepreneurs for producing the product, they charge the members to shop.

on a shelf, there were tariffs. The path from being in awe of those shiny green letters that, for me, equated success as an entrepreneur, making it in the natural foods world, and potential world domination to embittered, disgruntled entrepreneur took years and even some time in Whole Foods purgatory. Soon, we had two facings in ten stores. Then, three facings in twenty stores. I needed another flavor to get us more space, so that was when I decided to dirty up my chai.

BARACKTI CHAI

Traditional advice warns to keep politics out of business. Never comment on hot topics like climate change, abortion, race relations, or presidential campaigns. Never offend a potential customer because that is money lost. But I wasn't running a traditional business. New products came out of inspiration, not industry trends and conference rooms filled with data. I could have jumped on the pumpkin bandwagon like so many other American brands that shouldn't have—but I didn't. Even pumpkin pies have been ruined for me because Americans are bombarded with pumpkin flavoring from August to December. Not even real pumpkin but pumpkin flavors made in a lab. If the pumpkin lattes laden with sugar aren't shoved in your face enough, there's pumpkin cereal, lip balm, cream cheese, Pop Tarts, candy bars, hummus, SPAM, and even pumpkin condoms.

The first new flavor I created after the original Bhakti and then unsweetened Bhakti, was political. I started to drink Bhakti with espresso after I took a trip to Colombia. It was my first trip away without my kids, with my new boyfriend, Mark. He had just graduated with his PhD and was traveling for a few months in South America to celebrate. I met him in Cartagena, and it was such a romantic city to fall in love in. We went scuba diving in the Caribbean Sea, where I watched sea horses gallop by. We stayed up late, sipping tequila, smoking cloves, and playing chess on rooftop patios. And we drank Colombian cardamom-infused coffee every morning. *The creamy coffee warmth and fragrance of the cardamom would be the perfect backdrop to the ginger-infused Bhakti concentrate*, I thought. So, there was my third flavor to develop inspired by travel. On the label, I wrote, "Coffee and Tea? Together? The combination to some is like discussing politics and religion and could be sacrilegious for coffee and tea aficionados. But we believe in blending flavors for heated conversations aroused by travel. We use a cold-brewed technique to extract the unique smooth flavor from coffee that creates a creamy caramel backdrop to the warm gingery cardamom flavors of Bhakti."

Like most Democrats, I was in awe of Barack Obama. His intellect, swagger, talismanic speeches, and thoughtful policy to help low- and middle-income Americans. There was an enthusiasm for politics like I had never seen. I imagined it was like what people felt when JFK was running for president. Finally, a young, intelligent, compassionate, well-traveled, thoughtful candidate. I was inspired to volunteer with the Barack Obama campaign in my city by going door to door to register people and make sure college students turned in their ballots. Election night was electric. We cried, we danced, we rejoiced, and we drove around honking and screaming from our car. It felt like the new dawn of America. I was serving my new coffee chai (dirty chai) that night when a friend said I should come out with Barackti Chai. I laughed.

But the next day, I seriously considered what had been a fleeting joke the previous night. We could do it for the inauguration in two months. It could be my dirty chai but with cold-brewed Kenyan coffee, honoring Obama's father's heritage. We named it Barackti Chai—Inaugural Kenyan Coffee Blend. My designer

Terry superimposed Barack Obama's iconic Shepard Fairey image with dark blues and red for the label. I brought samples to the local Whole Foods Rocky Mountain regional buyer, and he loved it. They ordered it for the inauguration season as a limited edition. It even inspired them to hold parties in their stores with big-screen TVs televising the historic inauguration of the first African American president. I added the Tagore poem "Let My Country Awake" to the back of the label.[20]

I first fell in love with Tagore in India. I was touring the home (now a museum) of Indira Gandhi,[21] and this quote from Tagore was on her office wall. I wrote it in my journal that day, shuffling along with other tourists. When we walked outside, there, under an arch of bougainvillea, was the crystal plaque on the ground where she was shot dead in her front yard. I wrote it down because it felt like exactly what America needed, and now I was sharing a little more of my India travels in words.

The day Barack Obama was sworn in as our forty-fourth president, my team and I passed out samples in numerous Whole Foods stores around Colorado and sold hundreds of Barackti Chai bottles. After it was launched, the response was phenomenal. We were featured in the national press, had people from out of state asking to buy the bottles as collector items, and were requested to send it to the White House. I don't know if Obama ever tasted or saw my formulation, but he's a tea drinker, so I wanted to believe he tasted it and took a minute to read the Tagore poem. I

---

20 Where the mind is without fear and the head is held high; Where knowledge is free; Where the world has not been broken up into fragments by narrow domestic walls; Where words come out from the depth of truth; Where tireless striving stretches its arms toward perfection; Where the clear stream of reason has not lost its way into the dreary desert sand of dead habit; Where the mind is led forward by thee into ever-widening thought and action—Into that heaven of freedom, my father, let my country awake.

21 The third and only female prime minister of India. Her father, Jawaharlal Nehru, was the first prime minister after India won its independence. While he worked closely with Mahatma Gandhi for independence for decades, he and Indira are not related by blood. Her son was later also a prime minister and also tragically experienced her fate of assassination.

imagined a slow smirk coming across his face and then a few head nods before he was whisked into another presidential moment. Just that imaginary thought made me proud inside.

A month later, my phone rang. "Is this Brook Eddy?" the voice sternly asked. He announced himself as being from Whole Foods corporate offices in Austin, Texas, and he didn't like what he saw on the shelves in some Colorado stores. "We can't have political products in our stores," he said in a low tone like one of those disguise-your-voice computerized programs kidnappers use.

Oh no, I'm getting in trouble again by men. It reminded me of all those Bible camp pastors, bosses, and my grandfather—using a stern voice to let me know I was breaking some rule. But I never was the kind of girl to say sorry to men upset with my actions. So I responded in my salty tone.

"If someone doesn't like it, they don't have to buy it. Plus, he's our president now. It's not political or partisan," I reasoned. "If Republicans still don't respect him as our commander in chief, they don't have to buy our bottled tea drink, and we're willing to take that risk."

He didn't like my answer, and he didn't like the fact that I wasn't shaking in my Uggs with a Whole Foods buyer calling me out. I don't know if that damaged my relationship with Whole Foods, but the response from consumers was overwhelmingly positive, and it felt good to stand up for my product.

We sold out of Barackti Chai in ten weeks. The reward far outweighed the risk, and we were a brand standing for what we believed in, regardless of whether or not we isolated or alienated consumers. To this day, people mention with fondness those Barackti bottles and that limited-edition dirty chai. I was even at a Zen retreat center in Crestone, Colorado, writing this book, and a tiny little woman in her sixties, bald like all ordained monks, snuck up behind me and showed me the Barackti jar she had saved; she stores her dried nuts in it. And four years later, we did it again. We called it Barackti Chai Re-Election Blend!

With the success of Barackti, it was now time to innovate into a bottled ready-to-drink—not just a chai concentrate people had to prepare, but a blended iced chai. We needed to think big if we were going to bring Bhakti national, and while the concentrate business was good for margins and cafés, it was hard to explain and sample to buyers and customers. I wanted something people could open and drink on the spot.

One buyer balked when I told him I was launching the line in June for the summer. It was February. "You mean next June, right?" No. I did not. I meant in four months. There were no planning sessions, consultants with hefty price tags, or innovation centers to wait on—just the flavors and inspiration again, all wrapped up with my nod to traveling. Tea was my canvas.

In my kitchen, I began blending. Mixing soy, almond milk, coconut milk, and Bhakti concentrate. The creaminess of the soy went perfectly with cold-brewed coffee and concentrate. The coconut milk needed a little something. More spices or sugar? No, it was a toasted coconut I wanted. I was able to source this from Califia, the alt-milk giant. What about that mouth feel? This was something I learned from a local food scientist when I brought him samples to test. I didn't want to add thickeners or preservatives or junk that can be found on so many nutritional labels, so he recommend higher fat content: coconut milk and soy milk. Natural ways to get that mouth feel. He later taught me when I was developing our chai drinking chocolate that the "it thing" I was looking for was salt. Just a touch brought out the depth of the chocolate and the sweetness of the cardamom. We all know salt and chocolate harmonize with each other, but in a drink, it felt counterintuitive to add salt. But it does something else in a drink: it makes your tongue want more; it creates a mouthwatering sensation.

Once I finalized the recipe for the Iced Chai line, I sourced glass bottles. These were not sexy glass bottles, but they were cheap and available, and I couldn't afford to do custom glass at three times the price. I wanted to and drooled over some of the design options, but a custom mold could be over $150,000 up front. So I ordered the BBQ sauce stock glass bottles, and used labels to make it look Bhakti colorful.

I developed and launched the first iced chai beverage by that summer, and it was received with resounding praise. I learned later our cold-brew iced chai flavor was the first ever cold-brewed bottled drink at Whole Foods. I missed that cold-brewed trend though, now valued at over $500 million, and all the investment that came with it, by about five years.

A SISTER SALVE

Like most entrepreneurs and most mothers, I had to be nonstop. It took every last sip of energy, creativity, resourcefulness, multitasking, time, and thousands of hours of lost sleep to manifest my company while caring for my children. I did it all because there wasn't another option. I even had to break the law in the name of multitasking. One day Ryzen yelled from the back seat on the way to his soccer practice, "Mom, you're not supposed to text and drive," and I quickly snapped, "I'm not. I'm emailing and driving. Completely different animal." I'm not endorsing distracted driving, but there were years I felt every moment needed to be packed with multitasking to survive.

Women disproportionately spend more time on unpaid care and chores than men, even forty years after the women's liberation movement. When comparing countries, India had the largest gap, with women spending six hours a day managing home duties compared to fifty minutes for men.

What if the government just paid for childcare or camps or gave out motherhood stipends? Instead of all the tax breaks for corporations and billionaires, what about tax breaks for mothers? Or boosting the Social Security accounts of women so they could actually retire—or retire early with dignity? That's what we all really want for Mother's Day!

Women are told a lie. We're told there's a work/family balance destination we can reach, but we have to work hard to do it. More yoga and less overtime work? Saying no to volunteer or board seats to get more sleep? Not until men take care of 50 percent of the household/family duties will there be a work/life balance for women. As the wise words of Gloria Steinem elucidate, "I have yet to hear a man ask for advice on how to combine raising a family and a career." Sometimes balance doesn't arrive until we're forced to back away from the combat zone that is building a company.

I thought I'd been tempering all the stress with the right ingredients, my bag of tricks for work/life balance: friends, bike rides, wine, yoga, chess, and hikes. But the balance still wasn't really there, just the heavy sighs of stress controlled in the short term. I was not living my best life. I was overtasked, and I couldn't do it all. Madeleine Albright got it right when she said, "Women can have it all—just not all at once."

It can feel very lonely to be an entrepreneur. I never wanted to burden my employees with the perils of starting, running, funding, and growing a company. I couldn't saddle them with the fears of not being able to fund payroll or the stress of landlords bullying me. But my girlfriends took it all on. After a long and unbearable week or on nights filled with tears when I told them I couldn't do it anymore, my girls were the ointment I applied—a sisterhood salve.

After putting Ryzen and Veda to bed, I made my nightly commute to my home office. I dove into paperwork, looked over expense spreadsheets, reviewed financial documents my bookkeeper had uploaded, created marketing and sales materials, caught up on emails, crossed items off my to-do list, and created more lists.

This was also my social time, my office hours to see friends. My friends became a part of the Bhakti family I was fostering.

They always brought gifts when they came to visit me at night: chocolate, tightly rolled joints, packs of cloves, wine, cheese, homemade kombucha, takeout Indian, and pictures to scroll through on dating apps. Nights of stories and shrieks during the summer months would sometimes wake my kids up, and I'd have to say, "Sorry, we'll be quieter," as if I was the teen and they were my sleeping grandparents.

These sisters saved my life during those years of starting and building Bhakti.

One friend was a night owl like me and loved to swing by and pick me up so we could take a quick night walk around the neighborhood. Then, we'd go back to the office and sip on her flask of whiskey while we caught up.

Another friend always brought white wine and a funny story. She was also a single mother of twins and my life support on so many occasions when I felt I had no idea how to deal with it all. If she could also financially support and emotionally support her two children alone, so could I. One night, we fell off my couch laughing and crawled on the floor for ten minutes, replaying the story of the father of her twins showing up to their fifth birthday BBQ party empty-handed. She asked him to run out and grab ketchup because she was out, and people would be arriving in twenty minutes. He left, only to return ten minutes later with two handfuls of ketchup packets from McDonald's. I could so relate. He'd eat the hot dogs and burgers at the party and drink all the beer she bought, but he couldn't even spend the three dollars for a ketchup bottle or ever be the one to throw and fund a birthday party.

I couldn't have raised my kids, nor raised Bhakti, without the love, support, and comic relief from my female friends. It doesn't just take a village to raise kids; it takes a village of women.

RED ZINGER

With our iced chai bottles expanding across the country, it was time to bring our brand to the largest natural foods expo in the country, Expo West, or as some call it, Sexpo! This is where eighty thousand industry professionals converge in Anaheim, California, for one weekend every year. And there may be a few hookups going on.

Morgan and I slowly rolled into the side of the expo hall in a Penske twenty-four-foot refrigerated truck to unload. We missed the window to ship our iced chai bottles and our booth to the venue, so we had to ship to a dock in California, rent a truck, and bring it there ourselves. The first of many expo mistakes and lessons. First, we were told we couldn't bring the product through the back dock because that was for union labor only, and we weren't allowed. I drove back there anyway. We pulled in next to an endless stream of semi-trucks, a rumbling vibration as all these trucks idled, waiting to unload. I found a staircase to the docks and someone to ask about refrigeration for our product. They directed me toward endless ice rinks of refrigerated space overflowing with pallets of product.

I found a guy who finally agreed to give us some space in exchange for cash. I ran to the ATM and pulled out $400 of my own money so I could slip him bundles of twenties. Morgan and I began to unload, one case at a time, walking each down a long corridor to our pallet-size rental slab. We walked through aisles of alternative milks, creamers, yogurts, kombucha, tofu, and butter-infused coffees until we were at the very back, and our fingers were frozen.

Once we had our product protected and chilled, we started to unload the pieces that made up our ten-by-ten booth. It was simple: our logo bursting as our backdrop, a high-top table to set up for sampling, and dangling marigolds as if we were a tea stall in India. That was the extent of our booth. We were in the basement with what were considered the "younger brands."

Upstairs, it was another world. Architects had designed three-story Burning Man-inspired tree houses for a kombucha brand. An energy shot company had tiers of lightbox installations with flashing colors, EDM uncing in the background, and hired models in short skirts. Or there were the life-sized, modern, garish homes with living garden walls, vegetation, and white sectionals as meeting rooms surrounded by glass, so anyone walking by could see how busy the brand was hosting men in dark-blue suits. Brands doing $300 million in revenue built facades of farm stands—as if their products came from farmers markets and not industrial food plants. There was a life-sized ship passing out cornmeal rice flour kids snacks.

I was in awe. I had never been to a trade show before and couldn't believe it. I'd thought these were hippie brands, and here they were, flaunting their wealth.

We were forced to purchase flooring from the venue. A gross blue carpet that, along with another 1.1 million square feet of carpet used for the expo, would be pulled up and thrown out after the weekend was over. By then it would be covered in speckles of nut butters, gourmet ketchup, yogurt drinks, aloe vera water, Thai sauces, kimchi, and chai—this carpet was a reminder of the privilege and the waste, the dark side of the natural foods industry. We could have covered all of Los Angeles with that stained carpet. And all the backdrops and constructed sets were used for one year and then thrown away. The following year a new theme, a new product launch, a new marketing VP with a new marketing initiative, and a new round of investment to fund it all.

But once the show started, I couldn't help but think of my mother. There, among the thousands of young entrepreneurs like me, the suits representing private equity, and the buyers with their plastic badges turned around so no one knew if they were from Safeway, Kroger, Whole Foods, or Pepsi looking to acquire, were her gray-haired peers proselytizing about the wonders of apple cider vinegar, bone broth, and meat alternatives. They were the founders and the activists of the entire natural food movement. Co-op owners, natural product organizers, and ingredient suppliers only working in organic and fair trade—these were the food revolutionaries.

My mother had sat at her kitchen table in Glenwood Springs writing in the journal I would later own, drinking Mo's 24 and Red Zinger, the first two Celestial Seasonings teas out of Boulder, Colorado. And now, her daughter was becoming friends with the founder of Celestial Seasonings, Mo Siegel—a tea sage. He hand-picked herbs around the Rocky Mountains foothills for his herbal tea blends when he first started his company. Now, he graciously sat with me and talked about tea importers and the tea category to help an inexperienced, out-of-her-league tea entrepreneur.

While other children of the fifties, like my mother, roamed the US looking for communes, freedom, like-minded hippie communities, free meals, or spiritual enclaves like the Hara Krishna movement, they also dove into action around food politics. A sonar was pulsing from cities like Ann Arbor, Madison, Austin, Boulder, Burlington, and Berkeley, pulling in the youth with what became a mainstream $4 trillion industry—that all began, really, with small co-op markets and hippies. The entire organic movement is also attributed to hippies.

"The food Americans were eating in the 1960s resembled nothing that any civilization on earth had ever eaten before," wrote Jonathan Kauffman in his book *Hippie Food*. Our food and the flavors of our food were developed in labs. After WWII, the industrial food complex prospered. Pesticides were lathered on crops. Food was engineered. Preservatives were developed. According to *The Taste of War*, "Hundreds of pesticides were approved, including DDT, which scientists invented after they were researching a nerve gas." Four hundred new food additives were developed in the 1950s alone.

This made the condition ripe for food rebellion and natural food innovation. *Diet for a Small Planet* became the bible, and vegetarianism a religion. It changed the way millions of Americans thought about how their country looked at food for profit instead of nutrition, health, and the environment.

The hippies were right. My Depression-era grandparents, with gardens and canning, were right. Supporting local farms came back in fashion. But unfortunately, only 1 percent of food purchased comes directly from farmers or artisans associated with farmers markets—and only by a very specific, white, and affluent demographic, so it is large grocery chains that drive the food train in America. Walmart controls one-third of the entire US food supply! The private market again dictates what gets into the mouths of Americans. While we've seen the financial prowess and control of Big Pharma, its counterpart, Big Food, has been making food cheaper by ignoring nutrition and adding sugar, salt, flavorings, and stabilizers, creating millions of unhealthy Americans.

Even with all the advances in healthy food, obesity, heart disease, and diabetes all increased with the rise of Big Food. At the same time, Big Food began to make more money and invested more in advertising. One-third of the US population is now considered obese, and the number of Americans with diabetes has doubled, making more and more people dependent on Big Pharma.

I met people fighting against Big Food and Big Pharma at the expo. Steve Demos, the father of tofu in the US, also offered me guidance. Like me, he was inspired by his travels in India during the seventies, as India had the largest population of vegetarians globally—an estimated 40 percent of the population (in the US, that number is 6 percent). He had a dream to make America plant-based and started WhiteWave Foods in 1979 in Boulder, Colorado. He stirred tofu in a caldron with a paddle he made by hand for his artisan tofu. He sold those thick, wobbly cakes of tofu at the farmers market and local health food stores. Later, he turned it into soy milk and became one of the leading beverage companies in the world. We purchased the soy milk and almond milk in our iced chai blends from WhiteWave. His legacy was followed by Ben and Jerry's,[22] the Paul Newman brand,[23] Annie's,[24] and Sambazon.[25] Some of the oldest natural food brands are now owned by General Mills, Smucker's, Hain-Celestial, Hormel, Pepsi, and Coke.

In addition to the too big to fail wealthy corporations, it was now movie stars that had entered the category. It was annoying to work so hard and then have actors swagger in with their new

---

22 Ben and Jerry spoke their protest songs through ice cream and used their proceeds to support NGOs and social justice.

23 The Paul Newman Brand, which started with just a single salad dressing, gives 100 percent of profits to charity. Since 1982, they have donated over $550 million to nonprofits focused on children, nutrition, independent media, and veterans.

24 Annie's, a small macaroni and cheese company, used organic ingredients without all the filler and fuss of traditional mac and cheese, oozing GMOs and sodium. She sold early, but the new team helped seed the community and organic farming movement. A decade later, General Mills purchased Annie's for $820 million.

25 Sambazon, a red wine–colored beverage made of acai, brought awareness to protecting the Amazon rainforest, using its milky purple elixir as an educational tool.

sparkling water or canned tea beverage. I can't believe Channing Tatum, Blake Lively, and JLo were deeply moved to create a new beverage—but they took so much air in the room and buzz away from the entrepreneurs standing on their feet all day, losing our voices talking and sampling, and carrying boxes and boxes of product around those trade-show hallways.

That first year, Bhakti Chai felt so small and insignificant. But we were well received, secured endless new accounts, heard from fans that they loved us, and witnessed so many people take their first Bhakti sips and look up in amazement. That felt so good to know my creations were making people happy, and we were building tea evangelists. Years later, we crushed Expo West. We handed out mini iced chai bottles, temporary henna tattoos, hats, and Bhakti shirts. While this created a little buzz around the brand, our yoga event had people talking. We hired Michael Franti to do a concert with the yogi Janet Stone. Four hundred bodies breathing, holding postures, and then dancing and jumping up and down (strangely reminiscent of Hare Krishna's kirtan!) outside of the convention center. Franti's lyrics of unity and love like sermons. It was a spectacle, and that not only put our brand on the map, but inspired people. Throughout the weekend, people commented on how Bhakti was bringing Expo West back to its hippie roots. It would have made my mother proud.

BREAKFAST CALL

The next week, everything came crashing with one phone call at 7:30 a.m. as I was pouring sloppy oatmeal into Ryzen and Veda's bowls, making lunches, and getting ready to leave for work and take them to school. It was a number I didn't recognize, but I answered anyway. When he said his name, I knew exactly why he was calling. He was a family friend of Regan's. They called it heart failure. But I learned later he had a hand in it, drinking and taking opioids. When I hung up, I sank to floor with wails, tears, and snot. One of the smartest and funniest people I have ever met, now an American statistic. I must have scared Ryzen and Veda, but soon I pulled them down on the floor with me and held them tight while I sobbed.

It's a strange feeling to be shocked, sad, angry, and pissed while also somewhat not surprised and a little relieved because you knew this day would come. I had been worrying about this call since I went to Sierra-Tucson with Regan. I had feared this would be his trajectory. If only he had answered that day I called. If only I could have told him I loved him. If only I could have saved his life. I'm going to miss his thoughtful insights, his humor that cracked a whip at my ass. His softness of love and tenderness. The all-encompassing, all-accepting unconditional love—and now the bitter aftertaste. I'll miss his complicated and sometimes convoluted mind, the depression that strangled him for months and years at a time. While the addiction patiently waited until he hit bottom and gave in.

CHAPTER 6

PUSHKAR

Pushkar, India, 2002

"Travel isn't always pretty. It isn't always comfortable. Sometimes it hurts, it even breaks your heart. But that's okay. The journey changes you; it should change you. It leaves marks on your memory, on your consciousness, on your heart, and on your body. You take something with you. Hopefully, you leave something good behind."

—ANTHONY BOURDAIN

Pushkar was a place to fall in love. Not just with the gods, meditation, puja, Sri Hari, and myself, but with a drink that would inspire the flavors of Bhakti Chai.

Pushkar sits in the desert in the northern state of Rajasthan. It attracts pilgrims from around the world with its sacred lake situated in the middle of town. The faithful cleanse themselves with holy water, and numerous lakeside temples reverberate with music and chanting across the water. The lake is said to have sprung from a lotus flower dropped by the creator god Brahma in the middle of the desert for purifying purposes. Some of Gandhi's ashes were sprinkled in this lake after his assassination in 1948.

The first night in town, Sri Hari took me to a night café called Monkey Glow, a smoky, neon-hued jungle gym for adults. We sat on colorful pillows on the floor with Israeli travelers and sipped hot lemon water with thick ginger branches floating on the top. I would have loved a little shot of vodka in mine, but Pushkar was dry and vegetarian. It was a good thing it was, because it was there that I combined two drinks that would become the basis for Bhakti Chai. The lemon ginger tea didn't have tea in it, but it had the spice level I loved. I ordered chai to add to it for the tea and caffeine. So with Bob Marley humming in the background and people openly smoking hash in chillums, I poured cups of chai into cups of lemon ginger tea, spilling it all over the kindergarten-size table all night, and loved the flavor combo. Then I ordered without lemon, ginger hot water I would add to a cup of chai. This became my go-to drink the rest of the trip. More R&D for what was becoming my chai sampling tour.

The following morning, I meditated on the rooftop of my guesthouse, waiting in the cool morning air for the roaring sun to peer over the mountain. Monkeys paced around the rooftops with dangling question-mark tails almost dripping on their noses. I closed my eyes and sank into an hour of meditation. I didn't know the answers to all the questions I kept asking myself about my future, about my purpose—but like the monkeys, I could sit with the questions and know the answers would be revealed.

Meditation jostled my spirit, soaring me to another plane, where I floated and hovered above my old sluggish self that had been fettered to fear. Nothing was my concern; nothing needed my thoughts or my problem solving. I didn't have to worry about finding a job, finding my purpose, or questioning my love life decisions. My life was unfolding perfectly.

When you wander the streets of Pushkar, you'll invariably bump into a cow around the bend. They're sweet and attempt to move out of the way, but managing such big bodies in such cramped streets, you sometimes collide. I could almost hear them grumble under their breath, "Oh, sorry, sorry, excuse me." I always gave them a little pat and snuggle. Even after hanging on the dusty streets and lounging on the *ghats*[26] all day, the cows were still a pristine snow-white.

Shops in Pushkar were crammed with statues of endless gods and goddesses, Kashmir scarfs, blankets, jewelry, beads, tapestry, *Mad Max* shirts made with leather straps the size of dental floss you'd see worn at Burning Man, carpets, books, and chillum pipes. Dotted between the shops were gorgeous little mini temples for drive-through praying.

Later, Sri Hari took me to the quiet back streets, away from the vendors and buzzing mopeds, to see, as he put it, "an artist man friend of mine." We wandered on a dirt road to a tiny one-room studio and peaked in the window. It was filled with hundreds of paintings and a man named Suraj, who seemed to be in a trance with a thin paintbrush like a calligraphy pen, making beautiful orange strokes of Ganesh on thin parchment paper. I felt bad to interrupt, but Sri Hari seemed to make house calls to everyone he knew. Suraj was soft spoken and gracious, soon serving us small cups of steaming chai with a floating mint leaf on top—another variation of chai for my collection! This remover of obstacles plus-size elephant god Ganesh was so regal on the paper. There was nowhere to go. There was nothing to do. No appointments or Swadhyay interviews. No calls or emails. We just sat in the studio of an artist, watching him paint and sipping sweet mint chai.

The next morning, it was a cacophony of sounds outside my window: chanting, screeching, moaning, splashing, barking,

---

26 Flight of wide stairs leading to a lake or river that people hang out on, watch festivals, do their daily puja, have kirtan, wash clothes, smoke beeties, or lounge with friends.

bells ringing, and a faint meow. I flung open the blue doors of my windows to see hundreds of people below me on the ghats. Clusters of bodies everywhere. Some were bathing, baptizing themselves in the holy water in the bright early morning sun, while others sprawled in circles. One man was pacing back and forth, yelling, "Sita Ram, Sita Ram, Sita Ram," in the most monotone voice. Women sprinkled water on their arms or dunked themselves into the water and then sat twisting their saris dry on the ghats. Hundreds of marigolds bobbed in the lake, orange and yellow buoys, each holding a prayer. I couldn't believe this was my view. For my room, with three windows overlooking the holy lake, the price was 300 rupees a night, or two dollars. I shared a squat toilet and shower, but I didn't care. It was a room with a view!

The temple next door echoed with bell knocks every few minutes. People struck the bell as they entered the temple and again as they left. *Ding.* It sounded like a round of boxing starting, but this *ding* signified the beginning of a prayer, a vibration to reaffirm what was just on their lips and hearts. Some were brazen or beseeching with a series of dings. Perhaps their prayers needed special attention. Others just struck one faint ding. I loved this action around the sacred. A vibration, a sound, a motion—giving everyone around an echo of a prayer.

I wanted to bathe there with the women below and do my prayers, but I wasn't allowed to be alone. I had to hire a Brahman (the highest priest caste) to facilitate prayers and puja with me in the lake. The guest-house owner wouldn't circumvent this rule when I asked if I could go alone. Or when I asked if there were any women Brahman I could hire. Her response was blunt. "No. No. No. Women don't know the puja. It has to be a Brahman." Why did Brahmans get to own religious superiority? Why was it only men? Probably the same reason Catholic priests are the only ones allowed to hear confessions—patriarchy and dated religious talons still stuck in society.

I walked down to the lake, and an older man with a huge smile waved at me. He had cluttered, uneven teeth like cashews, but he seemed so alive and bright with love. He was dressed in all white and told me he was a Brahman. He had white hair and was probably seventy-five, with flat duck feet and deep-brown splitting toenails. He escorted me down to the water. With his hands in namaste, he looked deep into my eyes and said, "My name Gordonva. What is your name?"

I had to repeat it because I couldn't believe my ears. "Gordonva?"

The white-haired man who raised me, my grandfather, was named Gordon. He was in his late seventies, in great health back in Michigan with my grandmother, both worrying about me in India. My grandfather showed me a contemplative life of prayer, creativity, integrity, and looking for purpose. Unfortunately, he was later hijacked by the judgment, banishment of nonbelievers to hell, and intolerance of the present-day far-right Christian movement misinformed by Fox News. An entire generation of men turned. But his true soul was like Gordonva, with a kind heart full of a loving god wanting to help a tourist pray in the water.

Gordonva and I stepped around wet cow dung patties studded with birdseed and rice remnants that the cows happily cleaned up following puja ceremonies. We stopped at a table, and I purchased the puja "kit" for our ceremony: a dried coconut shell, a red thread, marigolds, rice, red powder, a tiny incense pyramid, and a mini banana. These small puja items were an entire temple economy in India, an estimated $40 billion. Primarily women were these temple entrepreneurs, working to gather and string marigolds, find and clean coconut shells, and assemble the rice, oil, incense, and sweets into a little kit. When COVID-19 hit, temples were shut down. Therefore, doing puja and buying puja items ceased, disproportionally affecting women and revealing that these spiritual entrepreneurs were not protected under the law.

I explained I wanted to wash with the women in the lake, so with one flick of his hand and his head at the same time, I was off. I was really getting this head wobble wordless language.

I descended the stairs into the icy water, a numbing cold enveloping my legs and arms. I stepped farther down to find the next step and then the next. The women next to me held a rope that led out into the lake. They handed me the line, and I followed them down farther. They began bobbing up and down, holding their noses, so I did the same. It was cold but very refreshing. My skirt was now soaked and plastered to my thighs.

I descended into the dark, cold water and prayed. *Thank you for this amazing opportunity and experience.* And then, *Guide me. Guide me.* I decided I needed to float a little and let my skirt free in the water. I lay on my back and floated. The bright sun felt amazing on my face. I could have floated all day, but I heard giggling. I stood up, and the women around me were busting out laughing. "No, No, Madam. Like this." They showed me how I was supposed to bob up and down—not float, silly! So, I bobbed again and again.

I pulled myself up the steps with the rope and squeezed out my skirt before joining Gordonva. He handed me the coconut to hold and started with a prayer that I repeated after him, "Om Nama Shiva…Om Nama Shiva…," and then some words I couldn't decipher. "Love to Krishna…Hare Krishna…Hare Krishna, Ram, love to Ganesha…love to Lakshmi."

Yes! Love to that bad fucking ass female goddess Lakshmi! That queen of abundance. That sage of plenty and rapture. She doesn't just represent an abundance of money but an abundance of all that's good in the world—friends, love, compassion, success, spirit, and family. I loved seeing her perched in a lotus with gold coins dripping from her hands on walls, painted inside autorick-shaws, and prayed to in temples. This was the kind of religion I could get into—honoring goddesses and praying to that energy for female abundance.

When I met Lakshmi in India, I saw a part of me in the divine. It wasn't just a man's religion of subjugation. It was no longer a god in the image of a man. I grew up with that man as being a sometimes vengeful god (flooding and killing the entire earth's population, save Noah's ark) or a jealous god (triggered by statues of other gods is the first commandment). I could get behind the service and justice parts in the Judeo-Christian Bible, verses around helping the poor, feeding the hungry, and not oppressing immigrants always struck me as the truth—the real point of religion. But in a book of 31,102 total verses, only 480 verses mention love, service, or helping the poor. That's less than 2 percent of the entire Bible.

Lakshmi is a goddess of giving and gratitude and doesn't have a malicious bone in her body. She is a god of celebrations. A pure light in her being. She is a god of guidance.

Then, Gordonva continued with the prayers. "Love to Push-kar. Pushkar is your home now. You'll come back home. Love to India." And then more I couldn't translate. "Love to myself. Love to charity," he said. What a sweet code to infuse into religion and prayers. I then promised to love and do more charity and to come back to Pushkar. Gordonva tied a red thread around my right wrist (because I was not married), rubbed red powder on my third eye, and put rice in my hand to throw toward the lake. He held both my hands together and looked into my eyes with a beautiful, loving embrace. He then handed me a mini banana as my Prasad blessed communion. I ate it in two bites. So sweet and satisfying.

I wanted to find a guru in India. I imagined a deep peace

from finally finding an enlightened being to be my guide. I read the stories of people like Ram Dass that met Neem Karoli Baba and fell into an immediate drunk love. I yearned for that type of clarity, knowingness, and love affair like Sri Hari had with his guru in Vrindavan. But it hadn't happened, and I started to think it wouldn't.

Are these gurus and sadhus really enlightened? Men have been telling us they are the enlightened ones. Perhaps it's that women don't have that grandstanding ego to call themselves enlightened or gurus, but have just as much wisdom and spiritual prowess—or more! Seems like just another distraction men are trying to wrangle and dominate. I believe we all have slivers of enlightenment and some more if they exercise those muscles of contemplation, intuition, and connection with the divine.

In the afternoon, Sri Hari knocked on my door. "Come, BrookieJi, I have surprise." He wasn't wearing his usual long skirt, tank top, and scarf, but had on jeans and a tight T-shirt. I followed him down the bright blue stairs of my guesthouse to the streets below. There, he had a motorcycle, and said to get on. I jumped on the back, and we swerved through the narrow Pushkar streets until they opened up and dumped us on a wide dusty road outside of town. He drove faster, and I leaned the side of my face on his back, feeling the warmth. We rode past miles and miles of orange marigold farms. It looked like heaven. We kept driving until it became drier and drier, the sun hotter and harsher. The landscape crackling and then sand everywhere. He finally pulled over, and we ducked into a dark tent to find someone Sri Hari knew. We were given fresh mango juice, and then, around the tent, I saw the camels. We were going on a camel ride!

It's not like getting into stirrups on a horse. The camel is on its knees, and I was hoisted up between the humps.

"Hold on," the camel man yelled at me, "and don't let go!"

Suddenly, the camel stood up, and I was thrown forward, like lurching on a bull ride. I held on and luckily, within seconds, was stable and high—very high—on the camel. We began our saunter into the sand. The sun was starting to set, and the sky turned a vermillion hue. Even with the nonstop slurping sound of the camel, the drool, the foamy spit, and the intense streams of piss interrupting the moment, they are such mystical creatures. Their eyelashes seemed to stretch on forever. Beautiful long strokes of lashes surrounding kind eyes. We shuffled around on the camels at sunset and then zoomed back to Pushkar at dusk.

Later that night, as we walked through the city, the lights were suddenly pulled from their plugs, and before the rumble of the generators began to crack, there was a pause between the exhale and inhale, a quick divine reunion again. It's one of my favorite moments of the day in India, when silence and darkness exchange kisses. Sri Hari reached for me in the dark street and pulled me in for kisses. What a perfect day. I was happy.

The next day, about the time I would have been meeting my friends for a happy hour back in Boulder, I headed to a different kind of happy hour in Pushkar. As the sun faded, a gold hue splashed over everything in the city. It was as if gold strands stood still while the brilliant light held its breath in the air, a calm motionlessness—the magic hour. And then the temple doors flung open, and *darshan* began.

With the deities unveiled and the candles lit, next the music started to waft into the streets during this magic hour of light. I wandered into the Radha Krishna temple. It was a light-blue three-story sliver, like a San Francisco house with balconies and intricate artwork on the outside. You could miss it if you sneezed. I'd never seen it before or noticed it, but walking down the street, the pounding bell and drum mesmerized me and pulled me in. As I slipped off my sandals, I noticed the dazzling stained-glass-lined walls with pictures of Krishna playing his flute surrounded by his consort Radha and other adoring women. Radha is the most famous junior wife because of Krishna's passion and connection with her, even though she was married to another man. He wrote about her and made music for her and spoke of their love like his love for God. I loved this scandalous spirituality.

The music was beautiful and brought a smile to my face as I walked closer to the altar and joined the other people swaying and praying. I closed my eyes and felt lost in spiritual plenty, nirvana, oneness, or the energy that drives people to speak in tongues. I wasn't even stoned. I opened my eyes, and the young Brahman in a peach skirt came toward us and began to sprinkle drops of water on us from a gold bucket he held. I felt a few drops land on my arm. Holy drops from blessed water. I had my eyes closed and continued to sink into the feeling of contentment—the sense of no time. Dancing to the beats of the drum. I was transfixed and transported again.

Then, suddenly my face was slapped with water. I opened my eyes, and the Brahman had emptied the bucket in my face. I was drenched—it was as if my face was sliding off my skull. My jaw dropped in shock. I looked around, and the women around me bowed and raised their hands to the sky. One woman whispered, "Great blessing." Luckily, I had a scarf to wipe my eyes and dry off pieces of hair around my face. I thought I saw a mischievous smirk on the Brahman's face, a "Welcome to my temple, bitch" look from his water face smack.

I learned this was another type of ecstatic worship, another bhakti devotion like what I experienced in my first temple with the Hare Krishnas doing kirtan dancing and chanting. The bhakti movement arose as a more playful devotion. Less of a worshipper and more of a co-conspirator.

"A Bhakti is not content to worship God in word and ritual,

nor is he or she content to grasp only in theology. A Bhakti needs to possess him and be possessed by him. He also needs to sing, dance, make poetry, paintings, shrines, and sculpture to embody in every possible way," wrote A. K. Ramanujan. It was a strange condition, this bhakti, this feverish thirst, this appetite always wanting to be satiated, a creative yearning to express devotion in action. I wasn't drinking all the holy water yet, but it was still dripping down my nasal cavity.

I started to understand Sri Hari's excitement at attending kirtan and catching a buzz during his happy hour. Now, I found myself looking forward to the morning puja and bathing in the lake and then my happy hour temple tours. As I hadn't been drinking in India and didn't miss it at all, my God and temple time became my new G&T cocktail every afternoon around five.

Through these spiritual actions, I found a love in God. A love of God within. Somehow in a small town in western India, four hundred miles from the Pakistan border, I found the home I'd been searching for since I was a child. From being hauled around with my mother hitchhiking to the quiet home of my grandparents to dorms and roommates—I finally sighed with relief that this was my home within myself.

I met up with Sri Hari later, and we tucked into a back booth next to each other in a small restaurant off the busy street. Sitting close to each other, we tore off pieces from the big crispy *dosa* the size of a jumbo crepe. Dosa is made of rice and lentils ground together to make a fine batter. It's then put on a huge griddle with ghee and fried up for a warm, crispy vehicle of any type of sauce or dip like dahl, spicy potatoes, veggies, and creamy coconut sauces. After dinner, Sri Hari insisted on introducing me to his favorite Indian dessert. *Malpur* is a silver-dollar pancake drenched in caramel butter. The warm, glistening sauce dripped off Sri Hari's fingers and onto my lips. He fed me slowly, trying to linger at my mouth and teasing with each sensual, dripping bite.

On my way back to my guesthouse, a pregnant pink moon burst out behind the mountains. It ascended quickly to find a spot like an ornament dangling in the sky. I couldn't control what was happening—a bliss and love overpowering within me, a natural ecstasy. I was starting to imagine staying and building a life in India. I had hoped India would unlock a part of myself, but something else was happening, this surging feeling of love and peace. I didn't expect God would want to shack up with me like this every day. I felt so alive, free, in love, and at home. I could see God in drag all around me. In the ladies at the water, in Gordonva, in Sri Hari, in the camels soul. It was a surreal feeling to see god everywhere.

After all the meditation and kirtan, all the hikes and lovemaking, lazy afternoons reading poetry, laughing, and teasing each other, Sri Hari and I were full-blown in love. Yet at the same time, swirling around inside of this love was the fear of getting stuck in India. Sri Hari kept hinting we should stay and be together in Pushkar, but I knew I couldn't stay, I mean, not for real. After all, I was becoming a devotee, but of what, exactly? I kept questioning, *Could I stay and be happy?* I know I'd ultimately be restless. While it felt so good, this wasn't supposed to be my long-term path, right?

Maybe I'd become a *gopi* and stay in India forever in the big heart squeeze of the divine. Gopis are groups of women dedicated to the devotion of Krishna. They exemplify the highest form of unconditional love and unwavering affection for Krishna or God by following the teachings and giving their lives to Krishna. During the time of Krishna, they would travel with him and follow him when he spread his message and played his music. Today, some call themselves gopis and live in ashrams for Krishna. I honestly could not do that.

Or I could find a job in India. I saw girls from Australia and Germany living in Pushkar, working at Monkey Glow, selling jewelry, or giving massages. I could do that, too, if I really wanted to make India my home and next chapter. But something bigger was pulling at me. I didn't know what it was yet, but it was telling me not to get too comfortable in Pushkar, or with Sri Hari.

I vacillated between seeing him as a life experience and wanting to make this last forever. I was falling in love. But my critical eye twitched watching Sri Hari's compulsive rules for puja (the rose petals, crumbly sweets, incense, feathers, holy water, pictures, and of course the crucial placement of all these objects in a methodical order for proper connection with Krishna), even while I continued to plummet deeper into love's lunacy. I knew we couldn't be together long term. He was being recruited for a holy man's life. He was auditioning for the guru part, and I was on a path toward debauchery, drugs, travel, many more lovers, adventure, and noncommitment. It could never work long term. Just like an impassioned conversation in Croatian he had with some of his Hare Krishna friends, I couldn't share the wonder and enthusiasm of Krishna with him. I didn't understand. I saw the beauty and love, but it wasn't a path I wanted to devote my life to.

SHIVA FESTIVAL

I couldn't believe my luck. I was in Pushkar for the Shiva festival, which is about getting high! Since 1000 BCE, bhang lassi has been the sacramental drink of India. It's made of yogurt, nuts, spices, rose water, and bhang, which is ground cannabis leaves; a marijuana lassi. The next week it was the Shiva festival, and we drank the green wheat germ bhang lassi, or at least I did. Sri Hari's cup was still full when I ventured to pour my second. We were at Monkey Glow again, and this time, it was all about letting go. The

Shiva festival permits twenty-four hours of excess and celebrates the light of Shiva. It's a day of reaching for the light and touching, through one's elevated senses, the light that Shiva has to offer.

It's similar to the Jewish festival of Purim,[27] also celebrated in the spring. The streets were vibrating with celebrations at every corner. Parades down the road, dancing circles, loud voices rumbling prayers over the loudspeakers, kids pounding drums, EDM at Monkey Glow, and chanting circles drifting throughout Pushkar.

I scolded Sri Hari for nursing the drink. Eventually, I could see him smiling a little more uncontrollably. Staring at me a little longer and with an internal giggle, but not going as far as I was headed. My head and I had to dance. I couldn't have controlled my perma-grin even if I'd wanted to. I spun, twirled, and danced, yet felt like I was floating. Everyone around me was in love, including Sri Hari and me. He joined me dancing and I could tell he was high like me. We couldn't stop whispering that we loved each other. It felt more potent than the drug Ecstasy.

Eventually, I hit that "find your bed now" wall after smoking a few too many beeties (thinly rolled cigarettes the size of a mini pencil used to mark your sushi order) and slipped out of a conversation with a French girl also contemplating staying longer in India. I wobbled, skipped, and swayed down the road while the dogs and cows lounged on the side, rolling their eyes at our silliness. I got back and sprawled on my bed just as the electrical cord was pulled, and the fan, lights, and sound stopped. When the male voices cracking and screeching from the loudspeakers

---

27   A holiday celebrated in the Jewish tradition—as a day of excess. Esther from the Bible wrote that it should be a day for feasts, gladness, and giving gifts to the poor. Alcohol is encouraged on this day, along with wearing masks to get out of oneself and falling into giddy excess. Both Holi and Purim fall around the same time on the calendar every spring, right before or during Fat Tuesday and Mardi Gras—also times to let go and let loose before the sacrifices of Lent.

ceased, and the techno music from Monkey Glow was unplugged, I suddenly heard the velvety voices of women in the temple below me in chanting circles for Shiva, the divine cosmic dancer. Bells dangling from their tiny, moving wrists, tambourines striking warm thighs for hours, massive sounds underground in mantras. I felt God smile. She was so happy with all of our joy. I, too, was smiling. I felt one with the universe, like we were all one family tree, interconnected and related.

Sri Hari came to check on me, and said, "Look who had a little too much bhang lassi." Even though I couldn't see his face, I could hear his smirk.

"I'm just stargazing," I said.

"Oh, I see, BrookieJi. With your eyes shut, and inside you see stars," he teased.

JAIPUR

After a month in Pushkar, I was still no closer to finding my purpose or path, but I was ready to make movement toward going home. I was starting to feel idle and anxious that I should be getting to work. That I shouldn't get too comfortable not working and creating more debt. I didn't know what, why, or when, but something was pushing me home to "get to business."

Sri Hari and I went to Jaipur, the pink city and the capital of Rajasthan before I traveled by train to Delhi for my flight home. We splurged on a nice hotel with A/C and spent a few days sightseeing. We toured the Wind Palace, Hawa Mahal. It's an ornate five-story palace built in the form of Krishna's crown, with 953 honeycomb-shaped balconies carved with pink lattice windows and tiny peepholes allowing the wind to stream through the palace and women to peer out. This was where the ladies of the court could sit and watch the streets below without being seen.

At the time, they strictly observed (or were forced to observe) pardah, which meant they couldn't be seen by strangers or appear in public. We sat in some of the concealed window ledges and watched the flurry of activity on the streets. I couldn't imagine being just a spectator to the craziness below. I would have wanted to sneak out and wander the streets like we did.

We went to the famous photographer who had a vintage wooden box camera on the streets below the Hawa Mahal and produced classic black-and-white images. With a sepia look (the real one from using the chemical process to convert metallic silver, not the sepia photo app), our photo showed us sitting down, leaning into each other, both with happy smiles on our faces. Two young kids (even though we were twenty-eight) in love and with our whole lives ahead of us.

We went to the grand Amber Fort and Palace. Constructed of sandstone and marble, it stands above the city and a lake with cobbled paths, countless courtyards, and a palace with twelve queen quarters (because the king had twelve wives) and huge public spaces where you could imagine grand balls and parties. The top floor housed the king's quarters and rooftop balconies, with the bottom floor for servants and concubines, because twelve wives couldn't satiate the appetite of the king.

Before we went out for my final Indian feast, Sri Hari took me to one last temple. This one honored the goddess Mata, which celebrates *hijras*, or third-gendered people. We sat down in the back of the circle already in motion with instruments and swaying to the chanting songs. We had another ecstatic temple dance night. It was exhilarating to see how these people spinning in saris with broad shoulders, Adam's apples, and five o'clock shadows were praised, not discriminated against. They are revered in India and hired to be at weddings, baptisms, births, and funerals, as their presence is considered holy. Similar to the Native American tradition of recognizing three genders, India is way ahead of Americans with inclusiveness.

The next morning, Sri Hari took me to the train station. Sri Hari was a guide and mentor, and I was so grateful to start my call to adventure with him when I arrived and then to end my trip with his arms around me again. We said things to each other over those months, volleying scenarios for a future together. I told him to move to Boulder, and he asked me to stay in India. Then he asked me to move in with him when he returned to Split, Croatia. At the time, it felt possible and exciting, but we wouldn't see each other again for thirteen years. He set my spiritual path on a new course, guided me to go within, loved me, and taught me so much about India. These meetings and phases in life with kindred spirits and lovers don't always mean lasting relations or marriage. But it did mean a lasting affair with India.

VICISSITUDE TRAIN

There's something empowering about sitting alone on a train in India. I could have re-created my entire life in one instant, getting off at any one of the stops and reinventing myself completely. A new name and new identity. Or turning around and staying in Pushkar.

Families sprawled around me, opening tiffins filled with folded naan and veggie curry. I rubbed my tan hand, and dirt crumbled off. When I scratched my head, my fingernails filled with crunchy soot. I didn't care. I felt alive. I felt so free. Nuclear bomb–like clouds formed in the distance above the palm trees, hovering cylinders, crystallized white clumps that I could almost swipe with my index finger as I waved my hand out the train window. Then the selling cracked through the corridor, "Coffee…coffee…chai…chai." I had to buy some. It was watery, but warm. I began to read the book Sri

Hari gave me. It was Hermann Hesse's *Steppenwolf.* I opened up the first page, and there was an inscription: *Every living being is like universe…to my beloved universe, BrookieJi. Love, Sri Hari.*

I sat in silence for hours, reflecting on my time in the Swadhyay villages—all that beauty and joy I was blessed to witness. What a dream come true. And then replaying those intimate moments with Sri Hari. After a few hours of rolling down the lulling tracks, I must have fallen asleep.

The train suddenly squealed, screeched, and clamored to a stop in the middle of the desert. Everyone held on as we lurched forward and looked around at each other. Once stopped, people began getting off the train, so I followed. I stepped outside in the bright sun, a dusty vapor of heat everywhere. A line of people stretched down the train, and men were looking under the train. Without thinking, I, too, glanced under my train car. A charred, bloody body lay curled and still just steps from my feet. I screamed and then covered my mouth as the instant tears and throat tightening began.

Death is always humming a tune around you in India. Whether it's the zooming motorcycle on the narrow streets about to wipe your legs out from under you, giardia squirming in that undercooked food, the lurching buses flying toward you in a little tuk-tuk without windows, or the ash of burning bodies floating in the smoky air. You can't look away from death in India, and now it was sprawled right in front of me. Men came toward me and also looked under the train. They started talking in quick-tongued Hindi, and then I heard the word *suicide.*

Heavy grunts flopped from their lips as they waved their hands in frustration around the train delay, and then one looked at me as if I shouldn't be upset. "Just another suicide," and then he clucked, "it's karma." What a fucking asshole. I hated this about men saying "karma" in India. I saw a horse on the side of road in agony with a broken bloody leg, and men just walked by and said, "It's karma." I wanted to scream at them.

Another contorted, burned body under the wheels of suicide. Suicide again tearing and jabbing at my heart with incomprehension, anger, and sadness. *Why?* I stuffed my scarf into my face and felt so alone. I looked around; there would be no ambulance, rescue workers, crisis counselors, or clergy to arrive. The emotional pain this man must have felt, flinging his body in front of a fast-moving train, knowing he would be pulled under its burning hot wheels. I was crying about tragedy and so much pain on this earth. I was also crying, thinking of his family, who would hold that pain forever. Thinking about his family hearing the news and wailing, like my family did when they received the phone call about my mother. I was crying for myself and the shock and sadness I felt when I first learned of my mother's suicide.

IT NEVER MAKES SENSE

In my twenties, I took a pilgrimage to her grave in Colorado and brought flowers, a dreamcatcher, and some candy valentine hearts I found in her boxes of things I inherited from her friends. They still had the words stamped into them twenty-five years later. *Crush. Love. Peace. Sweet.* I placed the flowers, candy hearts, beautiful stones, and shells around her grave, a little collage art piece for my mom. I unpacked the picnic I'd brought and spread out a blanket: cheese, Corona beer, crackers, chocolate, and berries. I knew it wasn't her bones below me in the coffin listening but her spirit I had been talking to all my life.

After I smoked too many American Spirit cigarettes and said goodbye to my mother, I drove to the Grand Junction public library and went to work going through microfiche files. I finally found my mother's name as a reference with two separate entries.

I excitedly took the numbers to the microfiche room, found the microfilm, and placed it in a reader. The article's title magnified in front of me: "Woman Found Hanging from Treehouse." I gasped out loud. I couldn't believe it. How did she even know how to tie a noose? My heart sank, and I felt so sorry for her.

Seeing it illuminated in black and white was surreal. *So sad someone had to find her*, I thought. *Did little kids go out to play in their treehouse and find her?* So wretched someone had to write such a tragic headline in the *Grand Junction Sentinel*. So heart-breaking that I was crawling around the floor of a house a few blocks away as she took such drastic action. Her breastmilk evaporating into her cells, and I would never touch her again. So sad we only had a year together.

The second number corresponded to a two-sentence obituary just stating she went to Michigan State University and was survived by a daughter, parents, two sisters, and two brothers. Satisfying in a way that her name was acknowledged in print, but how depressing her life was summed up simply in two sentences. I decided to write her the obituary she deserved.[28]

Now, many years later and miles away in India, I wondered if this man next to my ankles would get an obituary. Would his body be recovered and given a proper burning ceremony in Varanasi?

---

28 If you met her, you'd instantly feel a zing for life. Her bright green eyes flickered as she would tell you about a Buddhist lecture that day, her recent Tai Chi class, the shiny polished stones she discovered on a hike, or the wonder and excitement when her cactus began to flower. She loved to make apple butter, homemade yogurt, or banana bread and give it to friends and neighbors. She had a profound social justice pulse, became the first female mayor at her high school, and signed a Peace Corp referendum as mayor. After attending Michigan State University, she moved to Glenwood Springs, Colorado, to live a simple life, create community, and bask in Colorado's beauty. She worked at the vapor caves in Glenwood Springs, giving massages, and volunteered at the community youth center and the Glenwood co-op market. Her life's rulebook was dive in, take risks, taste it all. Once she convinced her four girlfriends to pack for camping and follow her up to a vacant cabin in the woods she had discovered. Five days later, they left it exactly how they found it. She loved poetry, Cat Stevens, Nick Drake, Joni Mitchell, Walt Whitman, Kahlil Gibran, and sipping hot Tang while writing in her journal by the big kitchen window in the morning. She was known for lugging around some of her most recent "collected found treasures," as she put it. In the last year of her life, she hitchhiked around the country with her daughter and suffered a psychotic break. She loved big. She laughed loud. Her work was done here. She had another assignment.

I learned more than three hundred thousand farmers had committed suicide since 1995, and many by train. India is an agricultural country, with around 70 percent of its people depending directly or indirectly upon agriculture. Rising temperatures, droughts, government policies, and the lack of public mental health treatment contribute to this dangerous epidemic of people throwing themselves in front of moving trains. Bank loans devastated farmers and their families with debt and no way out when the temperature continued to rise. Owing anywhere from 50,000 to 80,000 rupees ($800 to $1,500) in one year can propel farmers into despair, and, after two years of drought with loan sharks feeding on them, they do not see any other way out. I don't know if this man was a farmer, depressed, or heard the voice calling him home, but just like in America, suicide is on the rise in India. In 2015, to bring awareness around this issue and put it in the face of politicians and bank lenders, activists brought skulls and bones belonging to farmers who had completed suicide and piled them near Parliament in Delhi.

What drives someone to take their life is varied and comes in many shades of despair. Depression, bipolar disorder, schizophrenia, psychosis, addiction, anxiety, stress, shame, alcoholism, hopelessness, financial ruin, postpartum psychosis, chronic pain, illness, debt, medication, and mania are some of the reasons people choose suicide. Every day in America, over a hundred people take their own life. Trying to make sense of my mother's decision all these years has only gleaned the realization that it's beyond our understanding. Nothing makes sense about suicide. The only thing that I've seen make sense about suicide is that, as a result of decades of war in Afghanistan and women and girls not allowed to go to school, or work, or have freedom, they are attempting suicide under the Taliban.

Whether it's Robin Williams or Anthony Bourdain, when

someone in the entertainment spotlight takes their life, we all gasp and wonder, "How could they do that? They seemed so happy! And they had everything!" We talk about statistics and that we have a mental health crisis. Someone must be suffering so intensely even to consider suicide as an option. Hanging oneself or jumping off a building or in front of a train feels so violent; someone must be in such severe pain and darkness that it seems like a light at the end of the tunnel—a whisper of freedom.

When Anthony Bourdain killed himself, I was in shock. It was as if I was punched in the stomach again with my mother's death, and by Regan's death—and I had never even met the guy. It didn't make any fucking sense. Do they hear voices that tell them the next life or the next reincarnation will be more comfortable, filled with less suffering? Is there something in the brain that tells them today is the day to feel free? And they follow the directions of this voice, guide, angel, or demon? Decide to find a way—or do they just stumble across a stash of electrical cords and find a treehouse? Or hear the train horn coming in the distance and decide this is the train, this is the day? Or wash down opioids with bourbon. Or as Anthony Bourdain did, see a hotel terry cloth robe and think, *That belt can be removed, and freedom is before me?*

When I got that early morning call about Regan's death, the truth is, I knew at the time it probably wasn't just heart failure. When he was at his worst place, he told me he would never kill himself. That he had thought about it, he owned handguns. But he wouldn't do that to me because of what happened to my mom. But being estranged from him, his suffering couldn't pull him from that option because of me. The death rate by suicide has jumped 35 percent in the past two decades. Of all the people who complete suicide, 90 percent have been diagnosed with a psychiatric disorder, including my mother, the day before she jumped out of that bedroom window with me in her arms trying to escape involuntary hospitalization.

CHAPTER 7

HIGHS & HEARTACHE

Boulder, Colorado, 2015–2016

"Once having traversed the threshold, the hero moves in a dream landscape of curiously fluid forms, where he must survive a succession of trials."

—JOSEPH CAMPBELL

No one tells you how much money you need to build a brand—or to raise children. It felt like I was always hustling for money to keep the business running and my kids fed. First there was Reno. He had salt-and-pepper hair, a matching salt-and-pepper goatee, and muscular calves below his United States Postal Service blue shorts. He delivered my mail most days around 5:30 p.m., after the bank had closed and my Bhakti bank account was teetering on negative. It was a constant game of not ordering too many ingredients or too much packaging and not paying my employees' reimbursement checks until I could collect from accounts who owed me for chai. I had no idea how much growth cost, but there I was every month, drowning in the lack of cash flow—days where I watched checks bounce on top of each other, a sea of red. Bounced check fees accumulated, credit cards maxed out, waiting with bated breath for a check to arrive in the mail. It was all so unsustainable.

I drove around the neighborhood looking for Reno—up and down the streets until I finally spotted those blue shorts. I explained my panic, and he happily handed over a stack of checks that made me heave a sigh of relief. Then I raced to my bank, ripping open envelopes and endorsing checks on the steering wheel while I drove. In the back seat, Ryzen and Veda chatted away about their day in school and their requests for dinner.

He gave me his cell number, and I called him my slot machine.

But that was just money owed to me. I needed money for growth.

I had tried traditional lenders, like my credit union and national bank chains, trying to shove my P&L statement in their faces. "Look," I explained. "We're profitable. We have grown a hundred and fifty percent in the last year. We have Whole Foods carrying our products and need capital to fulfill those orders."

The question wasn't "Can we see the Whole Foods purchase order?" or "Can we see more about your accounts receivables?" or "Tell us more about this van or equipment you need to buy." Nope, the question was "Do you have a husband?" or "Do you own a house?" or "Do you have a father who could cosign on the loan?"

Seriously. A husband or father? Was it 1950? I wish I could say it was because of the housing crash of 2008 that made bankers clench their butt cheeks more, but it was always like this. While the banks were bailed out after the crash and CEOs got their multimillion-dollar bonus checks, I couldn't even get a line of credit for inventory or a loan on account receivables.

So, without a bank or dad or husband or rich uncle, I went back to the dry-erase board in my mind to brainstorm ways to keep the business going. I needed to ask everyone I knew if they would consider a loan or an investment in Bhakti. The problem was I didn't know many people who had money.

And then my guru arrived—clothed not in robes or painted colors but in a brown business suit. A few University of Colorado students reached out, asking if they could use Bhakti as a local company to pitch to their business class.

Three weeks later, they presented their findings at a business school pitch event. They invited me, and I sampled hot Bhakti Chai and met Praful. He was a tiny Indian man with a joyous smile he could hardly contain. After tasting the chai, he looked at me in shock. "How do you know how to make such flavorful chai?" he asked. "I haven't tasted chai this good since India."

Now, that was a compliment. When I explained the big news about Whole Foods and product innovation, he asked, "How are you handling all the growth?"

My voice caught and started to crack into tears, but I swallowed that down. No one had asked me how I was handling it. It takes you by surprise sometimes when someone genuinely inquires and you're having a heavy stress day. "It's exciting because there's so much opportunity. But the lack of cash is thwarting the business. I can't afford to buy ingredients because I have to wait to get paid from accounts, and there's no capital to grow, so I'm always on a tightrope."

"Oh, sounds like you need an investment?"

What was happening? This Indian angel appeared and asked if I needed money? We met the next week and with a man twice my age and half my body weight, I went over a presentation and reasons to believe in Bhakti and me.

"I'll invest twenty-five thousand dollars for stock in the company."

He was my first angel investor. They call them angel investors for a reason. Without them, companies couldn't grow, and I would have failed. They were the angels swirling around, helping entrepreneurs fund their dreams.

Although my Indian angel Praful was a beautiful strike of kismet, it wasn't enough. Distributors charged more fees, I had to hire brokers to get into certain accounts, increase my liability insurance, pay for an attorney to set up investment documents, purchase more equipment—the list of needs kept growing.

Four months later, orders continued at a serious clip. It was astonishing both how fast it felt and also how slowly it all happened. And this was when another soon-to-be mentor strolled into my circle. Ross was a traditionally handsome businessman with short black hair and a chiseled chin. Probably the type you'd see in a nineties frat movie. But he wasn't a douche. He was kind, supportive, smart, and funny. He was already a fan of Bhakti, and his wife drank it regularly. He was also an entrepreneur, so he could relate to my stress burden and constant fear.

Raising capital was not only about selling my vision for the company; it was about finding the people that invest in small companies. Ross helped me fill the room with accredited investors[29] he knew and was responsible for helping me raise $125,000 that year. Another favorite part of the hero's journey (aside from my favorite, the call to adventure) is the meeting of mentors and allies on your journey. They help keep you on the path and provide inspiration, sage counsel, and direction when you're lost. Think Dorothy stumbling across the Scarecrow; Praful and Ross were my Scarecrow and Lion that knew a path to Oz.

The occasional angel investor balked at my charitable contributions (my monthly tithing) or the premium ingredients I used, mansplaining that without these, the company could be making

---

29 People who could take the risk on investing and losing the $10,000 or $50,0000 or even $200,000, and it wasn't going to affect their lives or investment portfolios.

more money. But they were not my people. They didn't get my vision, and I wasn't going to change our DNA or recipe for a few checks from men who failed to understand we were trying to build a different type of business.

Little by little, month after month, networking event after networking event, coffee meetings and lunch meetings, follow-up calls, and follow-up appointments, I'd finally hear those prized words, "I'm investing." Opening those checks for $5,000, $10,000, or $50,000 provided the same thrill I had experienced gaining a new account or earning that AM/FM clock radio—winning.

PRIVATE EQUITY

A year later, I needed to find someone to write bigger checks. I had heard horror stories of taking money and losing control. John Mackey of Whole Foods had warned, "Venture capitalists are like hitchhikers with credit cards. As long as you take them where *they* want to go, they'll pay for the gas. If not, they take over the car and throw you out."

I was advised to hire an investment banker to help find me institutional capital, or private equity, to help Bhakti grow faster. I arrived in New York City to interview with a few investment bankers and see if they would take us on. We were still too small for most to consider us, but we were growing.

This was a world I knew nothing about. Big, swanky, sixtieth-floor offices in New York City with mahogany walls and women at reception desks, like it was still the *Mad Men* era. I felt inexperienced. I didn't have an MBA. Aren't you supposed to have an MBA?

My first meeting was with a man named Brian. He was skinny, pale, and in his mid-forties. So lean he looked sick. His gray suit fell from his bones, and I worried he might be dying—until he went on and on about all his Iron Man competitions. He barely smiled and seemed to act like I was wasting his time.

Then there was Doug in the San Francisco open-concept offices with a Patagonia puffer vest, a chunky, flashy watch, and a little more meat on his bones. He brought me into a room full of similar looking bros to talk about Bhakti.

I knew how to sell Bhakti, but I didn't realize I had to learn a foreign language: male sports business-speak. Did they teach this at business school or on the golf course? I had to decipher phrases like *full-court press*, *game of inches*, *punting it*, and *bush-league* in conversations. I wanted to create phrases like *give it a gut*, as in a gut check and *putting in the IT*, as in intention.

Both Brian and Doug passed, said Bhakti was too small for them and to come back when we were doing $10 million in sales. I was on my own again.

As I grew more confident, I realized not having an MBA may have worked to my advantage. I didn't have the paradigm of business rules—those rules that may be a burden. You don't have to follow the rules you didn't sign up for. You can't learn gut instinct, grit, self-reflection, or how to trust yourself. You need vision, not professors with business theories or cocky cohorts. The entrepreneur is an artist, and the canvas doesn't ask for proper business-speak. It doesn't call out of the ether about focus groups or what Coke should do for market share of the sugar category. It just needs a few bold strokes to start, followed by more vision and creativity.

I once attended a pitch conference where I had to get up on stage and had five minutes to make them want to invest in me. The audience was fifty or so men, maybe a few wives and other pitchers like me. I remember the spotlight glaring at me as I felt the heat rise to my face. I hoped my slides would click appropriately. I threw on my enthusiastic smile and dove into the data and "reasons to believe." They gave me business cards but no cash.

Another wasted night with a bunch of boring dudes. I was up against men who were pitching tech ideas with no proven customers or sales. They were only in the idea phase but somehow walked out of these rooms with millions and millions in funding. I had data. I had customers. I had a track record—but again and again, the answer was no. Or the answer was "Chai seems too niche."

"It's not too niche for Starbucks and the entire country of India," I would respond.

It wasn't that men were inherently sexist; it was the system. Men invested in people who looked like them. In people they went to college with, in people they golfed with and grew up with. A fraternity where money flowed between them and very rarely fell into the hands of women or minorities. Only 8 percent of women worldwide hold management roles in venture capital and private equity.

So, when I was trying to sell my vision and pitch my business, it was in rooms full of men, usually over fifty-five. And these pitch decks always had to have the word *disrupt*. That's what investors wanted to hear. We were all *disrupting* the food and beverage category, like it was AI or something.

I wondered whether my chances would have been different if more women were in the room. Women, after all, were my consumers and Bhakti's demographic.

I couldn't find any women investment bankers or women in the private equity space. The funding of women entrepreneurs was even more shocking. Less than 3 percent of all investment money goes toward women entrepreneurs. That number is less than 1 percent for women of color. If a company has male and female co-founders, as many husband–wife collaborations start, that number jumps to 17 percent of funding. So just the addition of a man to the founder team makes a woman more likely to get investors.

I was selling a vision that these investors were not familiar with. Yes, they knew all about the yoga craze (a multibillion-dollar industry) that they funded through the founders of Lululemon, Core Power Yoga, Athletica, and Prana—all male owned in the female-dominated yoga space. But they didn't seem to think there was an opportunity to convert all the Starbucks chai drinkers to Bhakti and, similarly, create a tea movement or a lifestyle brand around Bhakti. I imagined more women may have been able to spot Bhakti's potential if they were in the room.

I was surprised that all I had built wasn't getting attention like so many other beverage brands in my space. I knew that, with sufficient capital, Bhakti could become a $50 million brand. If water companies and coconut beverages could do it, I knew we could sell a good-for-you fresh ginger drink with caffeine.

Luckily, just as I was feeling discouraged, I was introduced to a local private equity firm devoted to impact investing. Impact investing is when investors deploy capital to generate social or environmental impact along with a financial return. They saw our B Corporation status, sustainable sourcing, zero-waste manufacturing, product innovation, and charitable donations as being just as imperative as our growth. They also said being a female-founded and run company was important to them. They, too, saw the disparity in funding women.

I met the principal investor of the fund, a slim, handsome man with salt-and-pepper hair in his sixties. While a seasoned business and private equity man, he also had a Colorado native sensibility, a little granola deep inside. He would become a great advisor, a friend, a challenger, a headache, and a teacher. I would come to see him as not just caring about multiplying his fund's investment (which he did), but caring for me and my future. He was another type of angel. Another mentor showing up on my path, now the Tinman joined the crew towards Oz.

The months before closing the first private equity deal were brutal. We were running on fumes, and I was doing my regular full-time job with an additional fifteen hours of work a week pulling all the due diligence documents together with the lawyers, accountants, and consultants. Weeks and weeks of back-and-forth negotiations, and getting every *i* dotted. As we approached closing, and they knew we were a month away from running out of money, their attorneys started to bite. Tiny little nibbles at our ankles for more power, more influence, and more standing in the company. My attorney and I fought back but had to concede on many items. They knew our debts and cash balances; they knew we couldn't let them walk away, or we would be out of business.

Soon, $3 million was wired to Bhakti's checking account. I had never seen so much money on the screen of a bank account. I could finally sigh with relief that we would stay alive now. I was in awe of what this investment meant. I could hire more people, invest in innovation and marketing, give my employees raises, bonuses, contribute to their retirement accounts, give more to our nonprofit partners, and build a brewery!

ROLLER-SKATING BREW CREW

The demand for Bhakti products intensified, and we outgrew our shared space. Out of necessity, I had to build our own brewery. No one in the country would brew tea, press ginger, mill spices, and package it all in glass bottles with allergens like almond milk, soy milk, and coconut milk, so I was forced to build a brewery from the ground up to keep up with the demand of our growing product lines. I never daydreamed of building a bottling manufacturing plant, like where Laverne and Shirley worked.

I was becoming a real manufacturer. Such an adult word. Images of car parts and Kellogg churning out cereal for the world, not my little recipe from my stove. When I was filling out all the loan documents for brewery equipment, I realized I was an American manufacturer. I was a job creator, following in the footsteps of centuries of enterprises.

Securing the brew space was another lesson in trust. It was scary to put my signature alone on those loan documents for brewing and bottling equipment. If anything happened, I was responsible for repaying more than $800,000 in loans over the next five years. I was now the proud owner of a bottling line, bottling capper, new ginger press, labeler, and a five-year commercial brewery lease. There was no turning back now. The new brewery was almost ready for us to move in. The bottling line was soon to be delivered, along with three one-thousand-gallon brew tanks, a new ginger press, and cooling blast cells.

Standing in that empty brewery, I was suddenly brought back to one of my first unofficial under-the-table jobs at a beer bottling plant in Detroit. My friend's dad worked for Falstaff Beer, and on Saturdays, we sorted bottles and put together cardboard boxes. At the age of ten, nothing felt better than holding those two crisp twenties in my hand as we drove home. That was a fortune back then. Strange to find myself creating a brewery, owning a bottling line, sorting bottles, and now again constructing cardboard boxes for glass bottles thirty years later.

Before the brewery burst with production and the smells of cardamom and ginger, I wanted to christen it with a party. The fifteen-thousand-square-foot brewery space was empty, so it was the perfect place to have a roller-skating party. We rented roller skates, bought a disco ball, set up speakers, had food and cocktails catered, and warmed up the space with the team's energy. After I did some skating, round and round the brewery floors, attempted the Shoot the Duck (briefly, but hearing some crunch in my knees, I quickly stood back up), and did some backward skating from my fifth grade Skatin' Station days, I sat on the side and watched.

There they were: my family, more angels. We made shirts with BREW CREW stitched on the back for everyone who worked on the brew team. Morgan was wearing a one-piece silver jumpsuit. Allison came onboard to help me with marketing, customer service, trade shows, sampling events, and our website. She was our hot blonde den mother, going above and beyond for everyone even when it wasn't in her job description. Even though she was a single mother, she had the love and energy to mother us all too. She was wearing an outfit reminiscent of Sandy in *Grease*.

Austin was an up-and-coming natural foods star. He had just gotten married and put the Bhakti crew at the farthest table in the back, knowing we would be the rowdiest bunch, sneaking sips from flasks at his dry wedding. Tonight he wore a wig and tight bell-bottoms.

Jacki was my first VP of sales hire. She was sculpted like an athlete and had that same muscular Midwestern work ethic. She took Bhakti into places I had never heard of—retailers all across the Southeast and East Coast. She was gorgeous in her Jazzercise outfit on roller skates.

My half-brother was there, roller skating in a Lucha Libre wrestling mask. I had just promoted him to the director of brew operations. They were all cackling, holding hands, skating in long confident strides, racing. Some had nibbled on mushroom chocolates. Some had ingested cannabis gummy bears. Some were sober, and some were sipping from the keg of beer. The family I had always dreamed of having was in front of me, and I was the matriarch.

I loved these people. I had always envisioned a certain kind of family, and now I was creating what I had so wanted as a child through my kids, friends, employees, and colleagues—my chosen family.

TOTES OF TEA

Seeing so much innovation at Expo and how brands pivoted and rolled out shiny packages of new items for consumers every year, I knew I needed to think bigger than just chai. And how hard could it be to do something totally different?

First, I played in my home kitchen, brewing up some of our artisan teas and adding juices and sparkling water. I added lemon juice to our black tea and ginger. I added lime and mango juice to matcha tea. I added mint and sassafras to yerba mate and cherry juice to our rooibos artisan tea. I was ready to have my employees and friends try these new teas. Just like the other innovations, the response was positive. People couldn't stop drinking them and wanted more, and so did I.

I brought samples in cute glass bottles to the Whole Foods global team in Austin, Texas, and pitched them on Bhakti Sparkling Tea. Before investing in something that big and expensive, I needed a customer. I needed a retailer that similarly thought they were delicious, refreshing, unique, healthy, and the perfect addition to their drink sets. Whole Foods said yes, they wanted the new line of Bhakti Sparkling Tea to launch in all their stores nationally. Now, I had to find a soda-bottling copacker to blend, fizz, and package it for me.

Four months later, I was walking into a production factory in the dark early morning with a nonstop drizzling rain. I was in Portland, Oregon, for my first sparkling tea line bottling run. My hair was tucked into a hairnet, and I wore clear protective eye shields and a white lab coat. The blending began at four in the morning. This was the only line time a small brand like Bhakti could secure. The hot-fill processing line next door was cooking and filling plastic bottles with viscous teriyaki sauce. Smelling that in the early morning made me nauseous. I couldn't wait to get my ingredients running and smell the fresh mint for the mate and the mango puree in the lime matcha blend. I was standing where Pepsi products were made. This felt like I had made it big time.

I couldn't wait to see the glass filled with my new creation on an endless conveyor belt of colorful bottles. As I was scheming what angle I would shoot the video from to send to my team to post on Instagram when the bottles began to shuffle down the line with our beautiful, bright labels, the plant manager came walking up to me in a fury.

"We have a big problem," he said. "Your totes of brewed tea arrived, but they did not have tamper-proof seals, so we can't use them." He had an impenetrable attitude, but I had dealt with worse.

I heard no all the time. Every day someone told me I couldn't do something. Pushing for the yes and being optimistic was ingrained in my nature. I convinced the "no" people 99 percent of the time to say yes. I would figure out a workaround. I was confident I could pivot this latest "no" script spewing from his tired mouth to a yes.

"We always have our totes sealed. Is there a way I can sign off on this, and we can use different seals next time?" I kindly asked.

"Yes, they were sealed, just not with a tamper-proof seal. Some-one could have opened the totes of brewed tea and compromised the integrity," he replied in a robotic tone.

"But no one did. They came from our brewery on a truck to your facility. Truck drivers don't tamper with products. Can we look into having them tested or signed off on by the trucking company, or I'll take the liability?" I said.

"No. Everything that we receive must have a tamper-proof seal on it, or we can't use the ingredient."

I pleaded with him to talk to the bottling plant owner to see if we could find a solution. We had just spent $70,000 to get all the ingredients, bottles, labels, and boxes there, and we were launching in Whole Foods in eight weeks. Dave, the bottling plant owner, was a sixty-year-old guy I'd convinced to give me a chance two months prior. He had said no then too. But after I sent him projections, flew out to meet with him in person, and assured him this sparkling tea line would be the next big product, he begrudgingly agreed—but only with an up-front payment and line time in the middle of the night.

My rational arguments, ideas for compromise, pleas for compassion, and lists of solutions didn't work. It was a rule they wouldn't break. Dave wouldn't do a thing. They would dump all of that freshly brewed organic and fair-trade tea—and charge us for it. They would also dump the mango puree and the fresh cherry juice that only had a one-week shelf life because they couldn't get us another slot on the line for another month. All of it down the drain with the excess teriyaki sauce. Which meant I had to go back to Whole Foods and postpone the launch, which meant we would miss the reset and paid promotion. Another $45,000 lost.

This was the "big time," and we had fucked up. First, I called the head brewer and asked what had happened. He had all the communication about product specs, timing, freight, and certifications needed for them to do our run. He used the tote seals we had on hand and didn't think the lack of a tamper-proof seal would be an issue. But that requirement was clearly spelled out on the spec sheet. Which was his job to read and follow. I wanted to fucking kick over cases of our glass bottles, a full-on glass-exploding temper tantrum. I wanted to roar and rage at him. But I wasn't that type of CEO. I never yelled at anyone. I often exhibited disdain or disappointment when things were not done properly. Or I got frustrated when someone missed an important deadline with a retailer. But I never yelled. Instead, I pushed it down, went out to my car, where there was still a dark, dreary rain, and burst into tears.

I drove to the airport to return my rental car and get on an earlier flight but had to drive around and around because I couldn't control my tears and my rage to get out the car and talk to the rental car attendant. Here I was again. Alone. Dealing with other people's fuckups. Having to salvage my company again. I knew I would have to tell my investors I'd just dumped their money down the drain. Literally. And I hate using that word, but they were literally dumping tea and ingredients down the drain. When was I going to get a fucking break? When was I not going to have all the stress on my shoulders? On a physiological level, every one of these dodge, pivot, fail, and cry moments of a startup ramps up adrenaline. Then the body secretes a hormone to constrict blood and heart muscles and stimulate the adrenal glands. These vessels begin to shred; the intestines and immune system all slow down to deal with this attack. Not the best daily practice to be doing.

I eventually had those sparkling tea bottles made and launched in Whole Foods nationally to great accolades and consumer enthusiasm. But this catastrophe foreshadowed how much Bhakti could fail and flounder and how I was just as powerless as I was saving those totes of tea. We were so fragile, like so many young companies, and the margin for error was slim. We were always just one crisis away from going under.

SCALDING

Bhakti was entering what I didn't know then was a pinnacle time that most entrepreneurs dream of. We were doing $6 million in revenue that year. We had money to fund growth and an industry taking notice of Bhakti. We were still small on many scales, and the pressure was to get to $15 million, but the brand had an awareness and street cred of a much larger CPG brand.

Buyers were calling us instead of us having to bang down

doors with beverage data to prove we deserved a chance. Edging out competitors was just as sweet as you might imagine after years of pushing and being overlooked. Coming up with seasonal products like Vegan Chai Nog and Holiday Chocolate Chai was exhilarating. It brought more press, more buzz, and like with the Barackti Chai, we sold out before the holidays were over.

We won Best New Hot Drink from the Fancy Food Association. It was a gold-plated statue of a chef perched on a base. My very first foodie Oscar. We were named Best Chai in the Country by the *San Francisco Chronicle* and I was nominated to be *Entrepreneur Magazine*'s Entrepreneur of the Year, making it to the top three finalists out of thousands of nominees. People recognized me from the local signs in Whole Foods, and the status was fun. I was becoming a little local celebrity. Peer brands and brands much bigger than us wanted to do collaborations, like doing a Bhakti Chai Yogurt with Noosa or a Bhakti Beer with Avery Brewing. Or creating a Bhakti Chai Chip ice cream. We sampled it with tiny sugar cones—a three-bite goodness of creamy cardamom-ginger-vanilla ice cream, dark chocolate chips, and a crunchy cone. A triumphant *ha* to all those doubters who told me chai was too niche. To all those people who said Bhakti had too much ginger for the American palate.

We purchased the first ever electric street-legal tuk-tuk in the country that year. We customized it as a sampling station, named it Ginger, and hired an army of demo girls and one tan yoga man to go on a national Tuk-Tuk Tea Tour, handing out Bhakti samples and Bhakti swag. We didn't take a page from the Red Bull playbook—we improved it. That one orange-and-blue tuk-tuk tooling around every major city was attention grabbing. If only we could have replicated that and, like the Red Bull can cars, had a fleet of tuk-tuks.

This was the time we launched our official online giving

platform called GITA: give, inspire, take action. We took our charitable contributions and funneled everything through GITA. We had a huge GITA launch party, with the GITA Giving logo as a charm on hundreds of prayer bead bracelets we gave out. We introduced the site by highlighting the organization Wello, which provides waterwheels for transporting water in India, significantly increasing the amount of water and reducing time and physical burden, which disproportionally falls on women and girls. We also celebrated another grantee, Warm Cookies of the Revolution, the world's first civic health club that encouraged civic engagement. We sent girls to school. We funded scholarships for women. We funded meals for schoolgirls. It was feminism in action.

But beyond the parties and celebrations, innovation, and new business, every day there were problems to solve—problems that came with a growing company and a family that felt, at times, out of control and dysfunctional. Employees accidentally opening the drain and letting five hundred gallons of hot, freshly brewed tea down the drain (this happened multiple times). Brewery employees fighting to the point that we had to install cameras. I had to watch, in black and white, a woman go after people with a mop handle or dudes in yelling matches, chests puffed out like high school boys. I didn't want any part of this. I had to fire people, reprimand people, and try to be a team builder when people were acting like assholes. I had to put my half-brother on probation and not have bias when employees came to me complaining about his work ethic and days of disappearing and mistakes that cost the company tens of thousands of dollars. I wondered, *Should I hire a therapist to help my randomly picked new family resolve these issues? Or was there some kind of HR firm that could help me manage the chaos?*

Then one morning, my cell phone rang, announcing a surprise FDA inspection. They came unannounced in military-style uniforms. They had come before, with clipboards or clutching file folders, in suits or long, navy Ann Taylor skirts. But today, they sent in the military.

What was happening?

The risk of a catastrophic food safety issue was the ultimate nightmare for any food or beverage producer. Not only could it kill someone, but it would create scars on a company and hurl it into litigation and bankruptcy. When people asked what kept me up at night, it was the thought of hurting someone or running out of money. *Was there a complaint? Did someone die?* These were my first thoughts. I've heard the horror stories of a little boy dying of *E. coli* from drinking a green juice or mass sickness from salmonella in nut butters. And with the brew crew making mistakes and fired employees being disgruntled, I worried it could be bad. Did one of the brew guys accidentally brush broken glass into our bottles? Did they fail to test a batch, and some fungus had grown in our tea?

The FDA piled through our testing records. They checked temperatures. They roamed over each product, batch, ingredient lot, and brewing log.

These weren't the kind of men open to small talk. By the end of the day, I knew no one was sick, and no one had died. Nothing about our product was damaged or tainted. I was curious why they had come with their guns drawn. We had private auditing companies like organic, fair trade, Costco, and kosher at our facility every year, but never an unannounced FDA visit.

I had heard rumors of competitors calling the FDA anonymously. Tales of price fixing, product stealing, weight fabrication, and companies falsifying nutritional panels. This was the natural products industry! Why would competitors stoop so low? It was starting to feel like the mafia—another dark side of CPG. There's enough to go around for everyone. We can all succeed. It's not as if there's a finite pie of opportunity, and we must steal slices from each other.

The main offenses the FDA wrote us up for were, leaving a back door open to the dock while moving supplies (potential for rodents to come inside), one employee had a goatee and wasn't wearing a goatee hair net, and they wanted us to do a study on our ginger. But those were minor infractions.[30] Investors immediately became spooked and wanted us to stop using fresh ginger, even though the FDA never said that. They thought it would be safer and easier. I kept aligned with my recipe and values and fought to keep using fresh ginger, and I won. But I was again fighting alone, and it jostled me back into combat mode, my cortisol levels through the roof. It was as if the FDA was told to come in and find a way to distract us. It took six months, tens of thousands of dollars wasted, stress, new systems, new paperwork, and a total distraction—for no real reason. In the end, everything stayed the same except it added more simmering stress.

DESPAIR

Shark Tank continues to highlight the deals that birth million-aires and make it look easy and glamorous, but that's just good programming, editing, and PR. They don't show the agony of founders dealing with the FDA, botched production runs and ruined tea, and running on fumes. The show fetishizes the celebrity-famous wealthy entrepreneurs like Mark Cuban as rock

---

30 While it's the role of the FDA to investigate and that type of regulation keeps us all safe, there was something inherently not fair about it. Later, that really sunk in when during COVID-19 the FDA watered down their reports at the request of Trump. They released the actual report they made on a meatpacking plant with multiple COVID-19 deaths showing the firm language they used to protect workers. But Trump and his clown car changed the wording to make it weaker and less safe. They wrote, "If possible, take employee temperatures" and "If possible, have masks available." It would be as if the FDA had told us, "If possible, test your batches" or "If possible, have employees wear hairnets and gloves." These were not recommendations. There always seems to be a double standard.

stars. People think when they read a "sold for millions" headline, it happened overnight. Or that the founder still even owned 1 percent of those millions. But 90 percent of companies fail, and if there is a sale, many times it's not the overworked entrepreneur who reaps the rewards, but the investors. Even those keeping their heads above water and surviving may be dying inside.

Depression is the silent partner to some, never showing up on the P&L statement. Psychiatrists call it "impression management" or "fake it till you make it," and my acting turned out to be exhausting.

I first learned to fake it as a child. I didn't know what to call those heavy sandbags the first time they fastened to my torso. Hopelessness and existential questions settled over everything. *What was the point of all this?* Soccer had been my spirit animal and my meaning. The goals scored, the fresh scent of grass as we walked out on the newly manicured pitch, the dew on those early soccer mornings with a tribe of girls I loved—suddenly felt like a chore. Everything was a chore. Nothing mattered, and nothing had meaning. I didn't have the word for it then. I just sulked inside and, on the outside, painted on a smile like ColorStay lipstick.

By college, when those episodes arrived in the winter, I had a term for them: *seasonal depression.* I had a therapist and strategies to help me get through it, my bag of tricks—exercise, journaling, yoga, hikes, friends, writing poetry, and meditation—the exact things a depressed person cannot do. But then, when they began to happen in July and August, we just called it depression.

I had my worst depressive episode after I came back from India.

After three life-changing months, I returned to Colorado, thinking clarity would be upon me, my purpose sitting there on a platter waiting for my return. All those expectations, stories, and movies were scrolling through my mind about life falling into place after a spirit-filled journey. Shouldn't my purpose be clear now? Wasn't everything supposed to be wrapped up nicely now that I'd finished my call to adventure?

Instead, I awoke to what felt like a far-off dream. In India, even with the cows loitering in the road, nonstop honking, bumps, pushes, long stares from men, squat toilets reeking of diarrhea, or the constant motion, I never experienced culture shock. But when I returned to Colorado, culture shock reared up. The spotless streets and conversations about hikes done, miles run, calories burned, dairy avoided, fat denied, gluten shunned, meditation logged, and dates secured. Cleanses, colonics, food allergies, and digestion ailments were discussed openly at dinner parties. It felt like while I was gone, people found physical conditions and food allergies as their new part-time job. Forget what was happening in Afghanistan; a new generation of gassy people with food sensitivities was emerging in Colorado.

Some of my sadness seemed reasonable as I missed Sri Hari and wondered if I'd feel that love and spirit again. I still missed Regan and wondered if we would get back together. Some anxiety was reasonable because I hadn't found a career and was working part time at a general store in the middle of an old gold-mining town. But this was depression that filled me after returning from India, and I was willing to try anything. I went to a sweat lodge and inhaled the cool dirt at my feet when I was overheated and wanted to run out. I prayed around those hot rocks and pleaded to feel like myself again and touch and taste that spirit I knew in India. The sweat lodge purified my pores and gave my complexion a dewy look for a few days, but it did nothing to relieve my mood.

It didn't make sense. I was so lucky to have traveled across the world, experienced a different culture, and fallen in love with its people, religion, vibrancy, and complications—and myself. I was a healthy, privileged woman living in the utopic town of Boulder.

How could I be depressed? But I couldn't shake the existential thoughts around how everything seemed random and pointless. That we were all just fooling ourselves with busyness, death was coming for us in a blink, and there was no reason for anything. Shouldn't we all feel this existential, with heavy hearts as war rages, refugees starve, little boys are radicalized to hate, rape, and kill, and climate change transforms our planet? I even wondered if it was a sign that I should return to India or find Sri Hari. I couldn't stop replaying the image of the man under the train.

A month later, after another sweat lodge, I was told I was "too open" by a Ute native man named Joseph Real or Beautiful Painted Arrow. "Your heart is heavy with an openness of the world. You need to close down to adjust to being in America." And with that, he prescribed me peyote.[31] We're always told to open up. Brené Brown teaches us to be more vulnerable, and yoga teachers guide poses to open our hearts—but I was being told to close it down? That was how I began my peyote psychoactive-guided trip[32] to cure depression and shut her down. To heal whatever

---

31 For over two thousand years, indigenous and native people have been using peyote for religious ceremonies and healing medicine. Peyote is a small cactus with bulbous, stubby mushroom buttons and contains the hallucinogen mescaline. The word peyote is said to derive from the word glisten or glistening. Peyote is considered the first psychedelic, as it was identified and studied long before LSD and psilocybin mushrooms. It's on the books as a Schedule I illegal drug (with marijuana, mushrooms, cocaine, and Ecstasy), but it's protected under the Native American Religious Freedom Act.

32 It looked like dry, chunky wheat germ, and I was supposed to have two heaping tablespoons. I gulped down the first dry tablespoon of wood shavings, gagging the entire time as tears began to fall down my face. I chased the second tablespoon with orange juice and went to settle in on my bed with my journal next to me. First, I felt the flu inside my cells. Achy neck, hot back, dry mouth, and puke were gurgling in my belly. WTF? I just gave myself the flu voluntarily? Lovely. Still, the hopelessness, sadness, and loneliness were there, settled in right below the flu. I felt so alone. I eventually did throw up, my body eliminating what it translated as poison. Images began to surface of my mother. Her long hair brushed over me. She was busy and distracted, but she was there—physically. Like a woman hosting a party, she was rushing around my room and mind and consciousness. She was happy—a hummingbird hovering and then gone in an instant. A quick glimpse and a quick buzz. I wrote in my journal the feelings of her around me. Safety, calm, busyness, comfort, unconditional love. She didn't say much, and I was disappointed we couldn't have a long conversation. She said, "Don't get stuck." That's the only thing I remember her saying. But I was stuck. That's what depression is. Even after the eight-hour peyote session, the hopelessness, sadness, and loneliness remained for a few days. But slowly, day by day, it lifted. By closing down, I could actually reengage with my life in Boulder and not be burdened with sadness. The joy of nature and friends and art came back.

dark voodoo had been cast on my spirit since returning home and to be reminded of God—the one I knew was inside but was always absent during depression. The one I knew was love. The one I knew was magical and smirking and had a sense of humor, and was justice. But it felt like she'd disappeared lately, like me.

So when depression knocked on my door again, this time while running Bhakti, I knew I needed a different approach. Sweat lodges and peyote weren't an option. This was something a weighted blanket or micro-dosing couldn't cure. For a month, I had felt blank and had been trying to push through. I couldn't wait it out, or find anything in my bag of exhausting tricks to do. The effort to get out of bed, let alone paint on a smile and be the enthusiastic, inspiring-leader CEO just about put me over the edge.

It was never related to stress—that was a constant. It wasn't associated with bad news or a string of miserable meetings. It arrived unannounced, a heaviness I always thought would go away. But then you sleep, and it's still there—week after week. Waking up to depression again and again is debilitating and especially after stress dreams of fighting battles, being swept out to sea by hurricane rivers, crashing planes, and hiding from Boko Haram warlords all night. All I wanted was happy thoughts and joy.

I had to pry myself out of bed and into clothes. Showering was painful. I had to psych myself up as I drove to work. Sometimes I biked to work, thinking that would help. It didn't. Like a good actress, I walked in and asked everyone about their weekend, teased people, laughed—but was exhausted by the interactions. There was no rhyme or reason. If only there was a free Sierra-Tucson for stressed-out, overworked, grieving, financially struggling, depressed single mother entrepreneurs.

I talked to my therapist about trying antidepressants again and tried a new one, bupropion. After a week, getting out of bed was effortless. After two weeks, doing yoga was possible. My face was no longer faking conversations with my kids and colleagues; the real me was starting to return. Instead of soldiering on, each day, things felt a little more hopeful.

My depression lifted completely a few weeks later. It was magic. I was myself again. It was not as if everything was perfect—I still had stress, a deadbeat ex that screamed obscenities at me on the phone weekly, and worry about the business and finances—but I felt funny again, sarcastic and energetic. I felt like I could really see people again and be present with my kids. I felt sexy and alive. I was thankful and saw the world as beautiful, not a negative vortex of existential dread. It was as if the episode had never happened, but I knew it might arrive again unannounced. Or at least another stressor would arrive without warning.

I REALLY JUST NEEDED A SPA DAY

Growth mode is an exciting time in a company, a rapid fire of new accounts, new distributors, national press, and new products. The sparkling tea line was getting lots of press and sales and we were all riding high on the success, and it was exhilarating. At that point, I had been running the company for nine years. I had twenty-four full-time employees.

But with success and growth came more stress. More to lose. Everything fell on my shoulders. I had signed my name and was solely responsible for lines of credit, equipment loans, and lease agreements. I needed to release my crunched jaw and feel some freedom. I didn't have an executive assistant or a personal assistant. I didn't have a co-founder. I also didn't have a wife. Unlike many of my entrepreneur counterparts.

I held the stress deep within my being, hiding it from my employees. They didn't need to know that unless I found new investors, we would soon run out of cash. I didn't need to burden them with woes and worries, like off-gassing. My job was to inspire, not leak onto them. So I kept it all tucked in, stitched in close with a smile on my face and enthusiasm on my lips. Until that stress burst one day and forced me to look at it on a screen.

It was a Sunday like most. Ryzen and Veda were up early, asking for French toast. My kids were sitting on the kitchen island, putting raspberries on their fingers like thimbles and sucking them off into their mouths. I first felt a tingling in my left arm. It moved up my arm with burning electricity. I shook it off, massaged my arm, and kept going. By the time the maple syrup was pooling in the middle of our plates, there was a weight on my chest. Resounding baritone thumps were going off somewhere in my rib cage. I took deep inhales and kept moving. The tingling continued, and the burn moved up to my neck. I shook my arm and clenched my hands as if maybe they were falling asleep. I felt lightheaded.

Within five minutes, I was back in my bed, trying to get whatever alien was moving through my body to pass. I googled "tingling arm with chest pain," and it read "signs of a heart attack in women." No fucking way. Was I about to have a heart attack?

I called my doctor's office and waited on hold for an on-call doctor. My skin was flushed and tingling, like I had overdosed on niacin. I sighed loudly and searched Google for more clues. "The Silent Signs of a Heart Attack: exhaustion, stress, lightheadedness, aches, and fever." *Oh, hell no,* I thought. The on-call doctor said to go directly to the ER. I had a friend come over and watch my kids.

The ER heart scans showed irregularities, and they transferred me in an ambulance and admitted me to the hospital across town for tests and surveillance. I didn't feel like I was having a heart attack. I guess the ambulance drivers didn't think so either, as we slowly rolled to the other hospital without the sirens on.

I don't remember much of the hospital except running on a treadmill in a paper nightgown with electrodes on my chest. It was called a stress test. I remember thinking, *Could they really measure my stress level? Will they see my constant state of fear and stress?* I was an athlete at one time. I played soccer until I was in my mid-twenties, ran the Chicago Marathon when I was twenty-seven, skied in the winter, hiked, and practiced core power hot yoga. Wasn't I healthy? Even though I had a fever and was weak and clammy, braless and pantless, I ran like it was televised. Chin up, breathing through my nose and out my mouth, visualizing the finish line. My mantra in my head was *You are healthy. You are strong. You are not dying.* I watched the screen above the treadmill recording my EKG wave patterns and knew that even if those slashes and scratches meant I was fine, I was not fine. I couldn't do this anymore.

I spent the night in the hospital. They pumped me with fluids, fed me, and let me sleep for what felt like days. The tests came back with glowing reviews—my heart was healthy. Perhaps it was a twenty-four-hour flu with stress-induced heart fluttering? Or maybe it was some unconscious call for the only type of spa day/retreat center I could afford at that time: an all-expense-paid-by-health-insurance reboot. They could never precisely tell me what had occurred. I did know something had to change around Bhakti, because I was not fine under it all. I had to figure out a way to step away from Bhakti and get off the stress treadmill.

I'd been trying to chant this work-life balance mantra for years—not to prove that I could have it all but rather that I could handle it all. But when the meticulously woven plans and stitched sutures to keep everything tucked in and sealed ruptured, I saw what a farce it was to work so hard for this balance. How close to the edge I was teetering. Elizabeth Gilbert explained, "The word *balance* is a word that we have to be careful of because it's another tool in the arsenal that women are using against themselves as one more thing they are not doing right."

Just as I envisioned Bhakti's success, I now envisioned my escape to a quieter, calmer life. But if I wanted to exit Bhakti, it would not be served to me on a platter. To make this work, I first had to find more investment partners so I could afford to hire a new CEO to take over my management duties but still get paid and consult to make Bhakti grow. I couldn't exactly quit. I was supporting my children by myself. I could hire someone else who could put in the long hours and take us to the next level of growth.

But first, I had to work harder than ever to make it happen. It was like how I sped, swerved around cars, and ran red lights to get to a yoga class on time, only to then be able to relax. I now had to figure out a way to sell all or a portion of the company or to raise capital to hire a CEO and take a break. Over the next six months, that was my new secret goal and part-time job. An international beer conglomerate had recently launched a fund to support nonalcoholic beverage entrepreneurs. They wanted to look at diversifying and getting into the ready-to-drink market in tea and coffee. I was fortunate to sell them on my plan of growth, and they invested.

I told my team the plan, and they were completely supportive. I interviewed potential candidates for about six months. I included my team in the search process. We even joked when a ripped 6'5" candidate left the office that we all wanted to climb him. He wasn't a fit to be the CEO, but maybe a lover. I found two people, but due to timing, it wasn't an option for them, and I was getting restless. I was referred to a woman from out of state who was willing to move, seemed good on paper, and was well connected. I liked her, and I liked that she was a woman and saw my vision for the company. Some advisors recommended against her, but I was impatient. I needed a break, a personal exit, and I was exhausted. I couldn't wait any longer. I hired her and started the process of stepping away. It took a few long months to get her onboarded. I wanted her to feel true ownership and gave her my office. The plan was I would work from home, but on a more part-time basis. I was technically the president of the board, so she couldn't do anything too crazy. Plus, we were aligned on growth and the path forward. Or so I thought.

CHAPTER 8

SABBATICAL

Vrindavan and Jaipur, India, 2017

"There are a thousand ways to kneel and kiss the ground; there are a thousand ways to go home again."

—RUMI

I knew I would see him again.

When I boarded that train and said goodbye to Sri Hari, I had that knowingness, I just didn't think it would take thirteen years and temporarily breaking up with my company to be able to find the time for a reunion. I was finally taking my daydream sabbatical from Bhakti that I had plotted and planned for over a year. I've always loved the word *sabbatical*, sounding so academic and also so liberating. I always wished our work culture provided these refresh options for professional and personal development. Or that our school systems provided passports and travel allowances for all high schoolers to give them a worldview lens in those formative teen years. While the number of US citizens with passports has increased in the last fifteen years, 60 percent of Americans have still never left the country.

The first month of not working full time was delicious. First, sleep became my devotion. All those years of being torn from a dream abruptly by Veda shrieking with a night terror or an emergency call from the brewers in the dark early morning because they had botched up the recipe and needed me to get them more emergency ingredients. I now knelt at the altar of sleep and couldn't get enough. Ten hours, twelve hours—I still didn't feel rested. I wanted more. Who knew there was such a thing as hypersomnia? Well, I had it and was proud to roll around in my bed with excessive sleep for months and recalibrate my cortisone levels.

Then, I had time to get back in touch with nature and with myself. Hiking up a path behind my house to open space (miles and miles of hiking trails), my stress evaporated. The *thunk* of the gate closing behind me, strong and decisive, signaled my escape as I entered my secret garden. The first ten minutes were all uphill, so the huff and heavy exhales knocked around my thoughts, loosening and unleashing lingering worries about the company. I tried to let go, but building something and watching others take it over and make decisions I wouldn't was a practice I had to learn. While I wasn't present day to day, I still very much monitored and tracked the business regularly.

What a blessing to have had that time to listen. To watch a summer storm roll in without doing anything but being there. How many years of summer storms did I miss building a company? Sitting in an air-conditioned office in the middle of summer, barely looking out the window. But now, I had the time to watch and listen. First, the trees become still and the birds are silent in one beat, as if suddenly muzzled, not a peep from one of them. Then, the random pings on the roof as the clouds transform before my eyes. Until those pings turn into bullets and the crash of thunder so loud the house shakes. The storm rolls in and out in twenty minutes and the birds begin to chirp again, the sun peeking through and reflecting on the glistening leaves.

My kids were starting middle school, and I loved being home and not stressed. Moe was in high school and would come home for lunch. We'd chat in the kitchen, and I loved being able to make him lunch, being there to listen. The endless conversations with all the kids in the kitchen were priceless. I held court around the kitchen island. If you stay in the kitchen long enough, that's where the teens and their friends end up. The conversations swirled around sex, alcohol, gossip, sensational news, drugs, social media trends, sports, and politics, and I was the moderator. I played Around the World at our basketball net with the kids without the nagging old voice thumping away inside, *Hurry up and throw the goddamn ball so I can get back to work.* The calm of enjoying each shot, enjoying the moment.

So many blessings dusted over me during that time of sabbatical. A new paradigm of what it meant to be successful. The success of being, the success of staring, the success of spending quiet time alone. Balance isn't a destination. But with my sabbatical, I found another part of myself that couldn't relax while being a CEO and raising children alone. It was the other half that Madeleine Albright said about women having it all—just not all at once.

My love of reading was reignited. Without spending ten hours a day on email and spreadsheet screens, I had time to actually read an entire book. And then another. And another. I was reminded of how books and my local library nourished me as a child. As an only child, I found new friends, boisterous sisters, exotic lands, and unexpected heroes in books. I rode my bike to the library and traveled to other worlds. In the summer, I always entered the summer reading contests and came home with ice cream gift certificates every week for finishing books. Later, I was recruited for the Book Bowl team. Reading lists of books and competing to answer questions. We even made it to the finals one year, competing against other library districts in the state. So it was full circle when I volunteered for the Colorado chapter of the Jaipur Literature Festival and was invited to attend the mother festival in Jaipur, India.

The Jaipur Literature Festival not only provides free events and literacy programs and supports libraries, but it puts on the "Greatest Literary Festival in the World." I saw how hard it was to get my kids to read[33] and knew this was becoming an epidemic, with too many screens and not enough written stories. I wanted to help spread the message that I knew as a child and was rediscovering on my work sabbatical.

But before I went to Jaipur for the festival, I planned to meet Sri Hari in Vrindavan. He had found me on Facebook a few years prior after losing touch for many years. That first friend request generated such a rush in my body. And then writing messages back and forth, his cute broken English, like, "BrookiJi, often thinking you in Pushkar" or a few weeks later, "Can I call you on Messenger to listen to your voice." We talked for hours that first time, reminiscing about all the stories, teasing, and sharing our lives from the last years. Then we FaceTimed, and seeing his face on the screen brought a little flutter of attraction and love. That's when you know it's a real connection—time has no barrier in the deep love and respect that was there. He was still living his bohemian Hare Krishna life. He spent the winters living in India then his summers on his parents' farm in Croatia. He had never married and was still living that spiritual life, teaching and practicing meditation. I shared pictures of Ryzen, Veda, and Moe

---

33   One in three teenagers have not read a book for pleasure in a year. The US ranks twenty-third in reading, with the average American reading five hours a week, versus India, which leads the world, with the average Indian reading ten hours and forty-two minutes a week.

with him and the Bhakti logo (which he loved) and pictures of all the products inspired by my learning about bhakti in India. He emailed me pictures of his dogs and cats in Croatia and of him on his travels in India.

THE REUNION

Landing in Delhi, the first thing I noticed was the smell. Walking out of the airport in the middle of the night, I thought, *Ah, the burning smell of India. So good to be back!* I know I'm not supposed to like the smell of pollution and torched crops and trash melding together because of the environmental ruin and countless lung diseases and all, but it felt familiar, and it felt like home. I stayed in a guesthouse surrounded by gardens. Quiet and protected with high stone walls and lumbering kumquat trees filled with bleeping birds and a few elusive peacocks. The perfect entry to India.

The next day, I ventured to the dusty, smoky, crowded bumpy streets of Vrindavan, where the pushes and pull of India began again. Delhi was India-light, with its manicured green spaces, spotless streets, and Uber cars everywhere. Compared to this town that was two hours south of Delhi but felt like I was stepping back in time. And those nonstop honks again!

The tuk-tuk slamming into potholes on dirt roads, knocking my ovaries loose each time we crashed down. Rats scurrying around corners. With standing water and sewage running along the roads, all the smells arrived again too. One minute its grasp your scarf over your nose from diesel, sewage, or the smell of mothballs, like urinal cakes in men's restrooms. The next minute, nag champa incense. *Ah, India! So happy to be back!*

Vrindavan is home to over five thousand temples and is said to be the place where Krishna spent time with his lover Radha. When I checked into my guesthouse, the welcome greeting was not namaste, or hello, but "Hare Krishna," sounding like *HA-de*. Everyone greets each other in Vrindavan with "Hare Krishna," and I liked the way it sounded on my lips.

I met Sri Hari in front of the ISKCON temple, a garish-looking mansion of white marble surrounded by a town of white marble, all within the temple gates. As soon as I slipped off my shoes, I looked up and saw Sri Hari approaching. It wasn't hard to spot him; he still hovered over everyone and had that high-on-God smile. He hadn't aged that much; I guess meditation works. Or not having kids, a business, work, or responsibilities!

"BrookieJi," he yelled, putting out his arms as I walked toward him. It felt so sweet to tuck into his tall frame again. My head could fit in his armpit. He was dressed less Hare Krishna devotee and more Hare Krishna tourist. He wore a tank top and flowy white pants. He still had his hair pulled back in a man bun and a hefty collection of prayer beads around his neck.

I felt nervous to feel sexual energy toward him and also uneasy that he would feel attracted to me and it would be awkward and unrequited. There was something there, a long-lost love, a long-lost friendship soul connection. But I wasn't sure it was a throw-down sexual hit.

We went to the center of the open temple, where a huge tree shaded a hundred or so people sitting around on the marble floors talking, eating, or in chanting circles. His kind of date. He got us cups of chai, and I looked around. *Oh, temple chai!* It was perfectly balanced. A touch of spice and sweet. There were hundreds and hundreds of people praying, chanting, congregating with endless smiles. This was not a Christmas Eve service; this was a Monday, and it happened every day there. We sat on the steps together and caught up. It was so good to see him, tease him, and just be with him. There was a little energy, a hint of a flame.

The ISKCON temple complex was like a small town. Over

a thousand people were roaming the promenades inside, with stores selling puja items, chai, food, and clothing. Smaller meditation auditoriums; chanting areas; courtyards; and a museum that housed wax life-size figurines of A.C. Bhaktivedanta. It was sweet to walk through the museum and feel like I was living in a time that, for hundreds of years in the future, would be honoring this holy person. Not a faraway rumored holy person like Jesus or the Buddha, but someone who had just walked the earth and created miracles, fed millions, spread joy, and changed lives. I was standing in the HQ of his teachings and followers.

We went upstairs and stood in a chanting line that weaved on a balcony surrounding one of the temples. There were 108 lotus flowers painted on the floor, and we began the ritual of stopping at each one and quietly reciting the Hare Krishna mantra. The holiest number in Hinduism is 108. I found that calming zone of saying it repetitively, my mind becoming clean of other thoughts than those words. Until it wasn't clean, and I began to wonder and picture if we would be lovers again, *Would I invite him back to my room? Did I want to make out with him?* Then I worried, *What if we don't have the same sexual chemistry we once had?* We grazed hands and bodies and did our 108 mantras, and I continued to consider this option.

We left the temple grounds, slipped our shoes back on, and walked through the alley streets of Vrindavan together at night. We stopped at a little fragrance store, sniffing different oils, and then a flower cart. We teased each other, and it didn't feel like we'd spent years apart. We were undeniably flirting.

Then, I felt something like a child scramble up my right leg, up onto my back, and land on my shoulder. I screamed and pushed it off with my right hand. I turned around and a monkey lumbered away, carrying the garland of red marigolds Sri Hari had just bought me that had been around my neck. This was not a little tree monkey; it was ripped and stocky. I was shaken, and my throat hurt from screeching so loud. But then, Sri Hari and I laughed as he held my hand to calm me down. He was always trying to be my protector in India, and here he was trying to do it again, but like that time at the bus stop after our beach day, he was again a little too late.

We walked back to my guesthouse, and it felt like a safe sanctuary away from the chaotic streets of Vrindavan, all the people in the temple complex, and the lurking monkeys. We had dinner at the vegetarian restaurant at the guesthouse, and it was filled with white people. German, Dutch, Australian, French—maybe disciples of Krishna, or those who had traveled there to visit the famous ISKCON temple. If they served alcohol (there is no booze or meat in Vrindavan) and I'd had a few strong margaritas, I could have invited him over for the night. But I just felt jet-lagged, tired, and asexual. My mind said no, and then my heart said no. I could have gone there, just to test it out, but the season felt like it had passed. There just wasn't that fire or forbidden fruit there may have been thirteen years prior. Or maybe it was because I'd closed that door on Sri Hari and couldn't find a way to open it just for a few days. Or it was just bad timing with the lethargic-can't-keep-your-head-up-after-7:00 p.m. jet lag. Maybe next time I'll plan to meet him a few weeks into my trip!

Our lives had gone in different directions. Sri Hari lives the life of a devotee. He eats free vegetarian meals at the ashram and stays there in a non-air-conditioned room for months. He doesn't have a paying job. I devour meat and alcohol. I love AC hotel rooms, especially the ones with spas and room service. I have a job, a mortgage, kids. But with all those differences in lifestyle, we can still have a deep love and deep appreciation. He still told me he loved me. And I told him I loved him, and meant it.

A few days later, I left for Jaipur, and Sri Hari stayed to sit with his guru. Another reason we weren't aligned. I couldn't imagine someone not wanting to go to a literature festival. Books—my most recent guru!

PINK CITY

The city was just as I had remembered. A salmon pink dusted over the old city, beautiful fabrics in every direction, stores full of parasols, gold bangles, wedding dresses, and jewelry. And traffic, chocked streets with endless autorickshaws lurching slowly in clouds of diesel.

I arrived at the festival, held at Diggi Palace, and was in awe. It was like Coachella for books. Five stages with five hundred to a thousand covered-in-linen chairs spread out over a huge property. Each tent was decorated with different fabrics and streaming colors. Book lovers from around the world gathered with Pulitzer Prize–winning authors, journalists, poets, politicians, historians, humanitarians, business leaders, and artists, all with the backdrop of a gorgeously curated outdoor festival.

The festival was five days, and over thirty thousand people attended. At night, there was live music on those stages, but I couldn't always muster going every night. I was lucky to be back in India, surrounded by books, making new friends, and also exploring the city with new eyes. As a guest delegate, I could also enjoy the special lounges for lunch and chai breaks, which were away from the crowds and a place to write and read. The chai was mild and lacked any spice, but I still drank it. Other than the temple chai with Sri Hari in Vrindavan, I couldn't find anything as fiery as my Bhakti the entire trip. I had been drinking my fresh ginger chai for so long now that it was strange to sip on chai that was more tea and sugar forward.

No India story is complete without a digestive account. I've got a gut of steel, so I always eat the street food—you must experience all the fried chaat with chutneys, like samosas or the thin and crispy pani puri with a spicy broth. I also eat yogurt or lassi every day to keep my probiotic count up. Luckily, this worked, and any digestive issues were cured with some activated charcoal within a few days.

That was until I stayed at my first five-star hotel in Jaipur. I became so violently ill I couldn't move my body. A fever, aches, and chills set in first. Then, I had to get to the bathroom but was so weak I thought my bottom half was paralyzed. I pulled my body to the bathroom with my forearms, an army crawl across the fancy French embroidered carpet. I didn't know which would happen first—the Poltergeist projectile vomiting or the *Bridesmaids* sink diarrhea; it felt like it could be simultaneous.

After a night of hell, I was finally able to keep water down. I shuddered and sweated under the blankets. At some point, I must have called the concierge desk asking for a doctor, and he arrived somewhere in one of my sweaty dreams. I sat up to tell him what had occurred, and he gave me some pills to take for three days. For the pills and the doctor house call, it was 500 rupees, or six dollars. It was hazy the next day, a creamy hot-milk film over everything, which made it easy to sit back and stare through my sickness. By day two, I could walk. By day three, I could eat toast.

Thankfully, this sickness occurred after the festival, so I didn't have to miss a minute of the show, full of inspiration and learning about new authors and changemakers around the world. I was inspired to tell my story on the page and couldn't wait to use my sabbatical time to write. I had no idea then my break from Bhakti was about to end.

CHAPTER 9

A ROLLING BOIL

Boulder, Colorado, 2018 & 2019

"Adversity is the mother of progress."

—MAHATMA GANDHI

My sabbatical came to an abrupt halt six months after I left the office and brought on the new CEO. They showed up at my door late on a Thursday night. My employees—Morgan, Allison, Jacki, Austin, and Denise—rolled into my kitchen and went directly to the cupboard for champagne glasses as if it was a celebration. But this was no celebration. It was a cry for help. A plea for me to intervene and save Bhakti. They opened bottles (but I could tell they'd all had a few before coming over), and we sat outside on my patio. Small talk, checking in, industry rumors.

And then Morgan spoke.

"Things feel like they are going backward, and we need you back."

I listened. Each of them took turns telling horror stories of long meetings with no direction, mixed messages, changing directions, ignored input, my vision reversed, funds drained on consultants. GITA donations slashed. A contract with a recruitment firm was left on the printer showing the CEO was looking to replace my team. Finding that contract was not the best way to learn they were going to be fired. I listened and felt sick for leaving them.

How could I be so selfish to bail on them? I was watching storms, sleeping in, meeting old lovers, and gorging on books while they had to deal with the stress I left behind and a new leader who wasn't working. I told them I would talk to the board, and I would come back more and help the CEO. I would make an effort to be in more meetings and have more face time with the CEO. I couldn't exactly rush back in and fire her. She had an employment contract, and we couldn't afford to pay her out.

The board advised to give it more time. They said this was common, and a transition would take at least a year. Within a few months of this late-night intervention, one by one, my original team was gone. And a new team, Bhakti 2.0, took the baton from us, only to eventually fumble and fall. Even though I came in more and tried to help the CEO and the new sales and marketing team, it was messy. I can see now there was a leadership vacuum, and the new CEO and I both trying to steer the ship wasn't working.

This new Bhakti 2.0 team decided to discontinue my sparkling tea line, funneling money away from supporting that and into developing a shelf-stable iced chai in plastic bottles. Then, some Bhakti 2.0 people were fired or left. The CEO hired more people, more consultants, and I barely knew anyone anymore. It didn't feel like my company. I felt impotent and powerless. I still put on my "taking one for the team" smile and tried to help. Tried to save our sales because we hadn't grown our revenue. Which was the entire point. Growth. And just then, there was some amazing press about me and the company—that turned sour.

CULTURAL FUNDAMENTALISM

I woke up and started scrolling through Instagram as usual. I posted on Bhakti's account a few times a week with some of our beautiful recipes or inspirational quotes. But before I could post, I was gut punched with hate. The week prior, *Inc.* magazine had published an article about Bhakti. It was exciting to have a national magazine highlight our work and brand. I had met the *Inc.* reporter at the Jaipur Literature Festival and pitched her on the idea to write about the company. The response was immediately positive, and it felt like some good news the company desperately needed.

Headlines are supposed to be clickbait to draw attention and be a little sensational. I understood that when *Inc.* titled the article "On a Whim, This Hippie Founder Packed Her Bags for India. Now, She's Made $35 Million Selling Chai" with a picture of me in all my white-girl blonde hair, sipping chai in India. It was sensational and untrue. The article later explained that the $35 million was the company's revenue since inception, not revenue for me, and nor was it profits. It also described there were no profits for the business; we were in the red. But not everyone read the article or knew about our giving programs and our partnerships with Indian tea and spice providers. They just saw the picture with the headline and started to roar online.

They accused me of stealing chai and appropriating Indian culture. The cancel mob was in full effect. Stalking, posting videos about how I stole chai and Indian culture, trolling, putting me down, saying my tea tasted like poison, posting death threats and bad reviews without even trying our products. There will always be haters, but with social media, it's numbing how mean people can be hidden away behind their screens and say such hateful things to strangers they know nothing about. Like Aaron Sorkin wrote in his adaptation of *To Kill a Mockingbird*, "A mob's a place where people go to take a break from their conscience." We've seen that at white supremacist rallies and on January 6, but it also happens behind closed doors with the mob of social media. Algorithms of hate coaxing people toward misinformation and separation.

Putting yourself out there in the arena[34] with the bullying and the really dark, violent threats thrust your way on social media is painful. I was told to die, commanded to shut down my company, told they were going to report me to Whole Foods and Amazon as a thief, threatened a spell that would be cast on me and all my employees, and warned to watch my back and watch my kids' backs if I didn't immediately apologize.

These were not Bhakti customers. These were merely lurkers who got riled up by seeing the article link on Twitter and Instagram and just followed along with the screaming voices without knowing anything about us.

With the history of human movement over the last three thousand years, not one group of people owns any recipes, ingredients, or food. Missionaries and merchants brought more than just Hinduism and Buddhism across Southwest Asia; they brought garlic, ginger, turmeric, black pepper, and tamarind. Then, Arab merchants and missionaries brought kebabs, biryanis, kormas, mint, and peppers, along with Islam. When forts and trading posts were established, European merchants brought with them Christianity, as well as tomatoes, potatoes, and peppers. In antiquity, Jewish

---

34 "It is not the critic who counts, not the man who points out how the strong man stumbles, or where the doer of deeds could have done them better. The credit belongs to the man who is actually in the arena, whose face is marred by dust and sweat and blood; who strives valiantly; who errs, who comes short again and again, because there is no effort without error and shortcoming; but who does actually strive to do the deeds; who knows great enthusiasms, the great devotions; who spends himself in a worthy cause; who at the best knows in the end the triumph of high achievement, and who at the worst, if he fails, at least fails while daring greatly, so that his place shall never be with those cold and timid souls who neither know victory nor defeat."—Theodore Roosevelt Good FN!!!

merchants sold spices, oils, and silks throughout the Middle East, Europe, and Africa (but did not try to sell Judaism).

Over the centuries, these ingredients were combined, and new dishes were created. Some called them curries.[35] No one country or people own spices or tea.

While many may have been well intentioned in voicing their concerns, they were somehow equating colonial business practices with a white girl making tea. The only stealing around tea was when those seeds were stolen from China, and history reveals that men of all countries, colors, religions, and races do terrible things for money and power. It's not just recent colonialism. We see this again and again throughout history.

The Indian columnist Palash Krishna Mehrotra wrote, "Those who are against cultural appropriation are nothing more than cultural fundamentalists." He wrote about a mob disrupting a performance of a white woman singing kirtan at Brown University, protesting her art as cultural appropriation. Mehrotra continued, "This type of protest is where the left and the right meet in cultural nationalism. The left's opposition to a white woman singing devotional songs is as right wing as it gets."

Was discovering a thread of inspiration—like a mantra whispering from another lifetime—wrong if it's from another culture? Who owns a culture, and who decides which culture we're allowed to belong to and what we're allowed to claim as "ours"? In an increasingly connected global and diverse planet, what belongs to whom? These are questions we should ask ourselves. I've

---

35 The word curry comes from kari in Tamil, which means a black pepper sauce. British colonizers misunderstood and called everything with spice by that name. When the French colonized Pondicherry, they created a milder version called vadouvan curry. After the British outlawed slavery in India, they offered free land to indentured servants after five years of service. Millions of Indians emigrated to other parts of the Commonwealth to claim this free land and took with them their cooking full of spices. They combined it with local ingredients in South Africa, Canada, Fiji, Australia, Jamaica, Singapore, and Uganda; that is how we have, today, so many flavorful and spicy global curry recipes.

never claimed to own the Indian culture; I'm appreciating, not appropriating.

I've never been to Norway, yet according to Ancestry.com, my great-grandparents came from Norway and Sweden. Should I have focused on starting a smoked salmon company because of my DNA results? Cardamom is popular in Scandinavia, as a result of the Vikings bringing it back from Istanbul over a thousand years ago. So was I allowed to use that spice? Is that how we're supposed to police innovation, inspiration, and creativity?

Literature, food, spices, religion, and philosophy come from the same earth we all share. Poets, sages, foodies, shamans, entrepreneurs, and garden-variety humans have unearthed elements from cultures that resonate with them since they could extract and drum on the skin of culture—appreciating and sharing the diversity of our harvests, spiritual traditions, musical notes, and art forms. All wanting to touch and taste the universal truth that we're all connected and link to this world family by sharing in these beautiful cultural jewels. This is sharing, not stealing.

Singing, dancing, creating, and innovating are not about getting permission. They're about adding to the artistic tapestry we are all weaving together in the present day. Even if there was some global body of culture to present an idea, song, movie, restaurant, fashion design, or tea company for approval, that would mean asking some nebulous group of men—because they have been the custodians of religion, culture, and trade and the gatekeepers of the three throughout history—for permission to be inspired by traditions.

I couldn't respond to each attack or slap. But I did respond to many, making my case. They did not like me offering my opinion. Many were shocked I wasn't apologizing. They demanded an apology. But I kept pushing my arguments that I didn't agree with inspiration as cultural appropriation, nor did my tea and spice partners in India or my Indian investors agree. I argued they weren't being forced to buy our products or to follow us on social media, so they could easily move on and find a new way to show shock and disdain. I wholeheartedly believe in boycotting companies that harm people, exploit the earth, enslave child workers, cheat people, or let executives sexually harass women, but acting out with such hostility for a woman making tea seemed like displaced anger—something performative and easy to do on social media, chiming in with the other tweeters to show shock.

More and more brands are apologizing to these bullies, and some people are even stepping down from public leadership roles. Most companies don't discontinue their products but have public relations agencies that respond to these complaints with apologies and contrition. This was yet another disagreement between the CEO and me: she was petrified during the few weeks we were getting attacked and wanted me to apologize. I refused.

I fell hard for India—the flavors, the sounds, the spirit, the people, the chanting, the landscape, the vibrancy, the smells, and the colors. Bhakti Chai was not appropriation; it was my love letter to India.

BK

The pace of the natural food and beverage industry has an insatiable appetite. It demands quick thinking, growth, and keeping up with innovation for the next big thing. Competitors were always nipping at your ankles while buyers were forcing you to get better velocities (sales) to keep your product on the shelf. It was hand-to-hand combat for shelf space. Considering these realities, the cold-brew coffee trend was exploding and breathing down our necks at this time. Four different coffee brands were nudging into our refrigerated shelf space, and we had no new innovation to fight back with. Combined, they had raised $70 million and could advance their cold-brew trend with national sampling, PR, influencers, celebrities, sponsorships, and marketing. Bhakti was sinking and losing shelf space—and relevancy.

I didn't realize I ran Bhakti from such a gut and trust place until I saw the next team take over. They spent months on focus groups, hand wringing, consultants, meetings, and analysis, which led to paralysis coupled with another year of declining sales. I don't think they understood the urgency the original, or OG, team had from our attention to nonstop growth to an ever-present awareness that if we were idle too long, we would lose. When I tried to intervene, they ignored my direction and my resolve. Retail grocery buyers need innovation every year to even agree to have a meeting with you, even if you already have a product on the shelf. What's the next big thing they can find and monetize? This is always the question. The reason my OG team accomplished so much—twenty product launches in ten years—was that we were fed by intuition, had an unwavering faith in each other, and had speed. We tasted, tested, reformulated, and tasted again. Then it was head down and bring it to market with a splash.

The board finally agreed, just eighteen months too late, and said I should start looking for a replacement for the CEO, which I did. I met with so many potential CEOs, but now our financials were even worse. We were hemorrhaging money and didn't have sales growth to show for it. No potential new hire wanted to take that on. It was looking like a sinking ship to them. I, too, was watching Bhakti capsize, soon to slip underneath the surface forever. Four months later, we were almost out of money, and our investors had made it clear—they were done funding a company without growth.

Our investors never asked us to be profitable. I know that sounds counterintuitive, but it wasn't an expectation among any of the growth beverage brands. Everyone in the beverage industry knew you had to spend excessive amounts of money to grow, fund customer trial (national sampling) initiatives, hire talent, expand nationally, build the brand, invest in marketing and social media, and then be acquired by a larger company that could work to make a product profitable with scale. And the money to do this all was from the company's investors. But without growth, that thesis spoiled. Now my investors were saying they couldn't fund losses, and the company couldn't fund itself on profits when they were losing $200,000 a month.

I was responsible for this. I'd hired hastily, stepped away too soon, and allowed private equity to say it was going to take time, which only made it worse. I pictured all the devotees blaming me for ruining Bhakti. They called Bhakti "Crackti" for a reason. I began to hear the whispers and rumors around town that Bhakti was flailing.

I had never uttered the word *bankruptcy* or even thought it would be an option. Not because I believed in some tale of its power, like bankers never using a red pen in business for fear of falling in the red. It never even occurred to me to discuss bankruptcy. I knew the statistics about 90 percent of businesses failing within the first five years. But not Bhakti. I only ever thought about growth. I thought all day and all night about improving and building—never the idea of unraveling my company or being in the position to salvage my company. I had a new realization—one that so many founders go through—the pain of your creation heading to a graveyard. It was heartbreaking.

We were a month away from running out of money, and the board started using the term *BK*, as if truncating the word took out the sting. I couldn't believe I was on calls discussing bankruptcy. I felt powerless. I didn't have the money or power to call for an emergency rescue operation. For so long, I had been the benevolent dictator, making the decisions. You can't run a company as a democracy when things move so fast and achieving compromise takes time. But this time, I couldn't call the shots or make decisions without money.

Then the word *insolvency* arose. How could we pay off our debts? Would the existing investors have to put in money to pay off the company's debts so they wouldn't be exposed? Would I? How much had I personally guaranteed, after all? I'd signed so many forms to ensure equipment and loans, and I had a sinking feeling in my stomach. How would I come up with the money to pay off all the debt?

I was on board calls with attorneys who worked in BK. Then more calls with buyers of distressed businesses. Would the investors "have a BK stain on their fund"? I sat on the phone with my jaw open. Even though I was on mute, I was moving my mouth, saying, "Oh my God...no fucking way...how is this happening?"

They uttered things like, "If we wind down now, perhaps a BK wouldn't be necessary from a legal perspective." They were already resigned to losing all their investment money. Millions of dollars vanished—no return on investment. No emotion. Nothing about the death of a beautiful brand I spent a decade building. There was never "These products are too good to fail." It was as if they were already planning the funeral and deciding on a wood coffin because it was cheaper. I was suddenly reminded of a Kabir poem:

> While you're busy perfuming your body with sandalwood,
> Someone else is chopping the wood for your funeral.
> A kite string in your hand, paan dribbling from your mouth,
> You forgot that when you die, they'll truss you up with rope,
> Just like the common thief, and put you on the pyre to burn.
> Can't you see that Rama is the only truth,
>   everything else a monstrous lie?

Bhakti was dying. First, I went to the bargaining stage of grief. I had to save my company. I wrote a Bhakti manifesto and sent it to the board and all the early investors and advisory board members. I'd do anything to get her back. I was going to fight the fight. I tried to find local investors to buy out all the current investors if they weren't interested in rekindling her. I met with the international beer conglomerate that had invested, begging for help. But they were dissolving their nonalcoholic focus, and those employees could care less for Bhakti. I searched everywhere for a white knight—a business term meaning someone who was willing to buy out the investors and give the company back over to the founder to run. Instead of having multiple investors trying to pull the company in different directions, there would be just one saving the company from bankruptcy.

What I really wanted was a goddess to arrive dressed in a sari and give me the funds I needed to take back the company. I paraded through endless coffee meetings with men. I showed them slides of the beloved brand I created, the vibrancy still coming through her even as the dismal numbers and scoreboard of defeat hung over every conversation. But there wasn't anything I could do. I was powerless unless I came up with millions of dollars overnight.

I went into the denial stage of grief or a type of disassociation mode. I stopped responding to Bhakti emails and just thought, *Fuck it* to anyone wanting me to do anything for Bhakti. I tried to put it out of my head like it wasn't crumbling. I had tried everything. I was powerless and pitiful, so I focused on my escape. On Airbnb, I found a Portuguese heritage home in Goa for $500 a month. I could sell my house and bring the kids to India. Have a funeral for Bhakti in Varanasi, put her logo on the pyre to burn, and let her go into the sky. I found a school for the kids and began to picture my new life. Monkeys swaying on trees in the backyard, three mopeds the kids and I would use to go to the market and the beach. Fuck this company. I couldn't save it, so I would take care of myself and move on.

Then, I entered the anger stage of grief. On hikes I would yell and mumble to myself, having imaginary conversations with everyone I blamed, including myself and everyone that wasn't helping me. Why couldn't anyone else see that this brand deserved to be saved?

The depression phase hit next, exhibited through isolation and alcohol. I'm not endorsing drinking, but I found it really did shift my perspective and stress. I was spending my days trying to get terms with our vendors to pay them in 120 days because we couldn't pay our bills and I was laying off people. Unraveling our business with distributors and trying to negotiate debt. This called for cocktails.

Finally, I moved onto the grief step of acceptance. The white knight or goddess in a sari never arrived to save my company. I had to accept the destiny now before me. I felt embarrassed that Bhakti was becoming another statistic of failure. Even in all the sadness, disappointment, fear, and mourning of my brand's death, I had the inner knowingness we would be all right—and I would eventually too.

I was supported, tethered, and suspended to some knowledge inside of me. It felt lonely dealing with all the fallout and my company crumbling, but I was not alone. I *am* not alone. I know deep down I've got this. Regardless of the surface circumstances, I am supported by something other. Supported by God, my mother, angels, Lakshmi, Regan, the divine, and knowingness. Yes, there will continue to be falls, stumbles, crashes, and death, but that thread of a spiritual support system is there.

The following week, our main investor, the Colorado granola native, called and said he had a plan. "If we sell the brewery effective next week, and all the brewery equipment, and discontinue the iced chai single-serve line, gallons, and all the glass quarts and growlers, I think there may be a way to save the company." I was helpless without money, and it was my only option. It was the last-ditch effort to save my company from bankruptcy. He would be willing to put in some capital if we were not burning money every month. Could I say no? The millions of iced-chai bottles consumed and used as morning caffeine pick-me-ups, afternoon treats, or after-yoga rituals would now be unavailable. More products and innovation in that natural foods graveyard. All those brewery employees let go.

He said some of the kindest words that I really needed to hear at the time: "Bhakti and Brook are a Colorado asset; we need to do what we can to build this company back up." He hadn't given up on us or me; he cared. Luckily, I didn't have to do it alone. The investor loaned me one of his young analysts to help turn the company around—for free. She was intelligent, hardworking, and a thoughtful blessing. Without her, I couldn't have gone back into the battlefield alone. See, I'm getting the hang of using these biz references!

The two of us worked together as a team to cut costs and build back sales. We pulled all spending and kept Bhakti going with a skeletal team and parched spending. I watched Bhakti do a series of rounds of chemotherapy. A plan so virulent it may just save her life. It was as if I was starting all over again. A mess to clean up. But at least I was well rested from my sabbatical days! It was like the early days before innovation or line extensions—Bhakti was back to just two products: the original fresh ginger chai concentrate and the unsweetened fresh ginger chai concentrate. All my other products swirled down that big drain of disappointment.

It was a season of uncertainty with the brand. There were days of stability and good news. New business with Costco. But then

COVID-19 snuck up behind us and our café business shriveled into almost nothing due to all the coffee shops shutting down, and our retail business dipped 25 percent. Luckily, our Amazon business kept us alive that year, as well as the governmental Paycheck Protection Plan.

I was learning another way to run a business. It wasn't as interesting or creative as when I was focused on new products and marketing campaigns. It wasn't as fun as buying an electric Tuk Tuk for sampling programs or hosting a Michael Franti concert. Now it was about conserving cash and working toward profitability. I had no other choice but to push the Bhakti boulder uphill again.

ON THE MEND

That summer, I went on my first eighteen-mile backpacking trip with three of my girlfriends. I needed to get out of the mindset of failure and into nature. We went to a place called Never Summer Wilderness because eleven months out of the year, it's either winter, fall, or a wet torrential spring snow. With our backpacks filled with tents, bedding, clothes, and camping food, we started on the trailhead and immediately found Never Summer was in its animated prime, a glimpse of magic. The wildflowers were in heat, flaunting their ripe peak colors and cheering us on as we pulled up the ascent. "You've got this," they whispered. Valleys of yellow St. John's wort lifted our mood subconsciously. We passed Indian paintbrush, stoic, erect, and regal dressed in crimson velvet, and aconite, a dangling, delicate purple flower that hid a poisonous secret. Tiny wild strawberries veiled behind blankets of green, melting in our mouths like a sweet sacrament, too small to even chew.

Around a bend I spotted a plump marmot sprawled, basking

in the sun. Butterflies skated around us at fifteen thousand feet. We climbed switchbacks in slow motion, gulping thin air. There was hope and tenacity everywhere we looked.

I didn't realize how hard the pack would be on my body. Old soccer and ski injuries pulsating and throbbing through my knees. Raw, bloody heels. Then came the splitting altitude headache. We made ski turns with our hiking poles, and my knees screamed louder for attention while my migraine hissed and throbbed in the background.

It's amazing what we can push our bodies to do—birth twins naturally, start a company alone with nothing, climb for days in pain with a backpack you want to throw off the cliff but don't because you don't want to lose your tent, water, or oatmeal packets.

As soon as I was feeling at the edge, one of my friends started humming the chorus to Cardi B's "WAP," and in a blink, we were singing it together. We giggled and cackled through the pain. Women heal and bolster each other. Stories, songs, silence—our mantras. Our sisterhood a sustenance serving us and the world.

It was an interesting way to celebrate summer after taking on the weight of another year with Bhakti, but it represented all the beauty and the pain packaged together. This new time of running Bhakti with no money and no fun marketing or innovation programs felt lonely. I didn't have my team anymore. I didn't have Morgan to laugh with about old men brokers in khakis farting during meetings or a team to brainstorm big marketing campaigns. It was all the boring business stuff of getting Bhakti stable.

But it's also what we can push our lives to do. What we can push our lives to signify. Looking ahead at that steep path and even farther to the pointed peak was dreadful. It was like looking ahead at Bhakti, starting over, and seeing all the uphill battles. But if I looked behind us and saw how far the four of us had traversed that day, experiencing the rowdy waterfalls and roaring rivers, berries, and laughs, I was proud. Just as when I looked back on Bhakti and saw all those products, parties, team building, fabulous friends and family, GITA giving, yoga events, and driving around in an electric tuk-tuk. I was proud.

Bhakti was all of it. Heavy lifting, joy, headaches and heartaches, pain, inspiration, spiritual winks and beauty, feeling out of control—all wrapped up in a chosen family. I found a home in India, across the world. I found a home in Boulder with friends and family. I found a home inside the company I built. I found a home inside of me.

At the end of those three days, we wrestled with our bodies, our spirits, and our thoughts—and we won. Whatever it took to get through the day, thinking about the hot water bottle we would sleep next to that night to warm our muscles (we called it our hot buddy) or stargazing on our backs together, the earth holding us tight, or the mirage of margaritas in the distance when we got back to the car and civilization. We did it.

There is no formula. No get-rich-quick, ten-ways-to-start-a-company manual. It's got to be in your gut. You have to want it so bad you'll sacrifice comfort for that dream of seeing it manifest before your eyes and the promise of freedom. You have to want to stay up all night finalizing product innovation in your kitchen or writing packaging copy because it's your creation. You have to tell yourself over and over again it will happen somehow, some way, but also know at the same time you will fail miserably. Be ready for failure bonfires along the way, or a big BK crash and burn.

It's constant uncertainty. For years, I clung to this idea that there were success milestones and then it would be smooth sailing. But it doesn't work like that. There are just varying degrees of unpredictability from paralyzed and pissed uncertainty to manageable and mediocre. It's what we all have in common in this experience called life.

I wish I'd had more impact—given more money to the Global Fund for Women and reproductive justice organizations, touched more farm workers on tea plantations in India or women in Peru harvesting our ginger—but I touched the world a little with my kids, my beverage, my brand, my GITA, my "workship," and my words. It was a purpose wrapped up not in one job but rather in one life and one message.

Bhakti is still bringing people joy with her fiery flavor and fresh ginger. Bhakti is resilient, just like her creator. Fifteen years ago, it all started with a Mason jar. This year, we're commemorating Bhakti's fifteenth anniversary by handing out chai—the same recipe that rescued me and gave me purpose—in Mason jars etched with our Bhakti logo and the Hafiz poem that still inspires me: "You carry all the ingredients to turn your existence into joy—mix them, mix them!"

EPILOGUE

Paris, France, September 2022

All the babies are grown. Ryzen and Veda are nineteen, Moe is twenty-four, and Bhakti is seventeen. I nurtured and strengthened them all, toughened them up with some adversity, took them on wild adventures, snuggled with them, and struggled with them. Motherhood is in itself a hero's journey, and I'm proud to have made it this far on that adventure. I have stretch marks—both physically on my stomach and side boobs from Ryzen and Veda—and marks on my soul from Bhakti, grief, and adversity. My house, once roaring with nonstop movement, toddlers growing into teens, arguments, laughter, and nonstop dirty dishes, is now still.

To celebrate dropping Ryzen and Veda off at separate universities and life *sans enfants*, I took myself to Paris for three weeks. I rented a little apartment with creaky wood floors, a kitchen the size of a linen closet, and floor-to-ceiling windows that opened up to a view of Montmartre. With the freedom of life on my own, I enrolled in cooking classes at La Cuisine. I ingested four sticks of butter learning to make caramel, béchamel, béarnaise, and port red wine and shallot sauce. I wandered through Shakespeare & Co.

bookstore, where Hemingway, Plath, Baldwin, and Stein hung out, dreaming that the book I wrote, an ode to all that Bhakti was and is, would be bound and on the shelf there one day.

I'm now sitting outside at a Parisian café. I ordered their house chai. It tastes like weak tea milk, without spice or sweetness. I can't drink it. I'll move on to wine. But it reminds me I still need to work on getting Bhakti to France. There are more places to bring Bhakti, more work to be done. Bhakti may need a few more years with her mother; she's grown but not yet ready to go out in the world without me. A pandemic and global supply chain issues, lack of cash, and manufacturing issues delayed her development. She's profitable and growing, but she's malnourished without investment. I want to find her a new home. Not abandon her like I did before, but give her a loving send-off. A place where she can be fortified with a new round of funding and innovation. I wish it were a Hollywood happy ending, and I could say I found her an energized team to make her an international brand while spreading the message of devotion and bankrolling thousands of nonprofit organizations. Or that I don't have to worry about Bhakti anymore, that she's out on her own and launched. But I can't say that.

There's some excitement of not knowing what will happen with Bhakti and my career, love life, travel life, and creative life. The possibilities keep me engaged and open to all potential prospects and suitors. There's a liberation in not knowing but also knowing it will reveal itself eventually. I'm supposed to continue to lead Bhakti and trust it will grow stronger. Finding the worship in the work as Swadhyay taught. Finding those pauses to enjoy the gifts that starting Bhakti gave me in between the uncertainty of the future.

A bus comes barreling down the street, spraying me with a gust of warm exhaust inches from my legs, and I'm reminded of all those buses in India. Back then, I wondered and worried so much about my future. About not living a full life or finding a family or a career path with purpose. But I created the chosen family I always wanted; I created a livelihood based on flavors, giving, and connection to something larger than dividends. India inspired my entire life, and look what came of that! Perhaps my next muse will start on the streets of Paris.

RECIPES

HOW TO MAKE THE BEST CUP OF CHAI EVER:

- 1 cup Bhakti Chai Original Concentrate
- ¾ cup oat milk or 2% milk
- Heat and sprinkle with ground cardamom

HOW TO MAKE THE BEST ICED DIRTY CHAI (BARACKTI CHAI) EVER:

- ¾ cup Bhakti Chai Original Concentrate
- ¾ cup oat milk or creamer
- ½ cup cold brew coffee
- Pour over ice

HOW TO MAKE THE BEST BHAKTI PALMER ICED TEA:

- ¾ cup Bhakti Chai Unsweetened Concentrate
- ¾ cup lemonade
- ½ cup sparkling water
- Pour over ice

ACKNOWLEDGMENTS

It takes a tribe to build a company, and to write a book.

First, a big cup of steamy gratitude to my Bhakti team that worked tirelessly for years to build and grow the brand, tendering incredible energy and enthusiasm every day. Thank you, Morgan, Alessandra, Jen-ai, Gabe, Beau, Dennis, Lori, Terry, Amy, Allison, Austin, Jackie, Denise, Ian, Susan, Kialah, Matthew, Alex, Pete, Scott, Kelly, Gaby, Amber, Grace, Mark, David, and Vanessa. Thank you to all my business supporters, investors, cheerleaders, and mentors throughout the years. Infinite gratitude to Ross, Peggy, Praful, Joan, Keith, the Weissman Family, Alan, David, Doug, Sylvia, Bob, Kevin, Jacob, Ryan, and Jim. You all offered so much guidance, support, inspiration, funding, and enthusiasm for Bhakti and me personally, even when it was risky.

Second, I'm grateful to those that directly helped in bringing *STEEPED* out into the world. Thank you, Sophie, AJ, and Sheila, at Lioncrest for guiding this book process and thank you Delia for believing in this project. I am also thankful to these dear friends that took the time to read and study early drafts, offering productive feedback, insights, and inspiration: Colleen, Jonny, Beth, Morgan, Jeff, Rosalind, and Mark.

And finally, those closer to my heart and home: To my bonus

mother, Kathleen. Thank you for loving me like a daughter, being sassy and worrying about me like a mother, devoting time and love from the double stroller days to the college years with the kids, and being a best friend wrapped up in grace and guidance. To my sister wives, a big squeeze of appreciation for the decades of comic relief, late night wine counseling sessions, road trips, night walks, rum smoothies, hikes, encouragement, and unconditional love: Thank you Korrie, Carol, Colleen, Selina, Jill, Morgan, Keele, Glenn, Tasha, Sarah, Dennis, Gail, and Jennifer. You were all the best cheerleaders for the brand, for Brook, and this book—even when they all didn't look like they would survive. Thank you, Scott, for being the kind of big-hearted brother every girl should be blessed to have. And most of all, thank you to my witty, thoughtful, supportive, and loving children: Veda, Ryzen, and Moe. You may think this is just my covert way of making you read a book, but I owe so much of my healed heart and happy home to you three. I'm humbled that the gods linked our souls and we could be family in this lifetime. I hope these stories inspire you to travel, question, persevere, be curious, search for your purpose in strange places, surround yourself with inspiring lovers and friends, and elevate the world while chiseling your own destiny and life.

BIBLIOGRAPHY

Bhaktivedanta, A. C. *Bhagavad-Gita as It Is*. New York: MacMillan, 1972.

Campbell, Joseph, and Bill Moyers. *The Power of Myth*. Edited by Betty Sue Flowers. New York: Doubleday, 1988.

Dalrymple, William. *The Anarchy: The Relentless Rise of the East India Company*. London: Bloomsbury, 2019.

DNA Web Team. "Let 'Kirtan' Carrie Sing." *DNA India*, last updated May 18, 2016. https://www.dnaindia.com/analysis/column-let-kirtan-carrie-sing-2213314.

FMI. "Supermarket Facts." Accessed April 27, 2023. https://www.fmi.org/our-research/supermarket-facts.

Frankopan, Peter. *The New Silk Roads: The New Asia and the Remaking of the World Order*. London: Bloomsbury, 2019.

Frankopan, Peter. *The Silk Roads: A New History of the World*. New York: Vintage Books, 2015.

Garfinkel, Perry. "Delivering Lunch in Mumbai, Across Generations." *New York Times*, February 2, 2017. https://www.nytimes.com/2017/02/02/jobs/dabbawalas-india-lunch.html?searchResultPosition=1.

Gibran, Kahlil. *The Prophet*. New York: Alfred A. Knopf, 2020. Originally published 1923.

Giridharadas, Anand. *Winners Take All: The Elite Charade of Changing the World*. New York: Vintage Books, 2019.

Gokhale, Namita, ed. *Mystics and Sceptics: In Search of Himalayan Masters*. India: HarperCollins, 2023.

Goldman, Seth, and Barry Nalebuff. *Mission in a Bottle: The Honest Guide to Doing Business Differently—and Succeeding*. Illustrated by Sungyoon Choi. New York: Crown Business, 2013.

Hafiz. *The Gift: Poems by Hafiz, the Great Sufi Master*. Translated by Daniel Ladinsky. New York: Penguin Books, 1999.

Hanushek, Eric, Shreekanth Mahendiran, and Chirantan Chatterjee. "Unintended Consequences to Education for All: India's Right to Education Act." VoxEU, CEPR. July 23, 2020. https://cepr.org/voxeu/columns/unintended-consequences-education-all-indias-right-education-act.

Jayapal, Pramila. *Pilgrimage: One Woman's Return to a Changing India*. Seattle: Seal Press, 2000.

Kabir. *Songs of Kabir*. Translated by Rabindranath Tagore. New York: MacMillan, 1915.

Kauffman, Jonathan. *Hippie Food: How Back-to-Landers, Longhairs, and Revolutionaries Changed the Way We Eat*. New York: William Morrow, 2018.

Lal, Malashiri, and Namita Gokhale, eds. *Finding Radha: The Quest for Love*. New York: Penguin Books, 2018.

Lorr, Benjamin. *The Secret Life of Groceries: The Dark Miracle of the American Supermarket*. New York: Avery, 2021.

Lutgendorf, Philip. "Making Tea in India: Chai, Capitalism, Culture." *Thesis Eleven* 113, no. 1 (2012): 11–31. https://doi.org/10.1177/0725513612456896.

Mackey, John, and Raj Sisodia. *Conscious Capitalism: Liberating the Heroic Spirit of Business*. Boston: Harvard Business Review Press, 2014.

McCloskey, Deirdre N. *Bourgeoise Dignity: Why Economics Can't Explain the Modern World*. Chicago: University of Chicago Press, 2010.

McMillan, Tracie. *The American Way of Eating: Undercover at Walmart, Applebee's, Farm Fields, and the Dinner Table*. New York: Scribner, 2012.

Neimark, Jill. "Yes, America Has a Working Tea Plantation. We Visited It." *The Salt*, NPR. August 23, 2016. https://www.npr.org/sections/thesalt/2016/08/23/488817144/america-s-only-full-time-tea-taster-talks-about-life-on-the-charleston-tea-plant.

Pettigrew, Jane. "American Tea Growers: Part 1." *Teforia* (blog), Medium. September 26, 2016. https://medium.com/@teforia/american-tea-growers-part-i-8c223b1d7fd8.

Pettigrew, Jane. "American Tea Growers: Part 2." *Teforia* (blog), *Medium*. September 26, 2016. https://medium.com/@teforia/american-tea-growers-part-ii-5358b71c772c.

Rilke, Rainer Maria. *Letters to a Young Poet*. Translated by M. D. Herten Norton. New York: W. W. Norton & Company, 2004. Originally published 1929.

Roosevelt, Theodore. "Address at the Sorbonne in Paris, France: 'Citizenship in a Republic,' April 23, 1910." The American Presidency Project. Accessed April 27, 2023. https://www.presidency.ucsb.edu/documents/address-the-sorbonne-paris-france-citizenship-republic.

Rose, Sarah. *For All the Tea in China: How England Stole the World's Favorite Drink and Changed History*. New York: Viking, 2010.

Rumi, Jalal al-Din. *The Essential Rumi*. Translated by Coleman Barks and John Moyne. San Francisco: HarperSanFrancisco, 1995.

Schwartz, Steve. *Art of Tea: A Journey of Ritual, Discovery, and Impact*. Lioncrest Publishing, 2022.

Sengupta, Hindol. *Sing, Dance, and Pray: The Inspirational Story of Srila Prabhupada Founder-Acharya of Iskcon.* India: Penguin Ananda, 2022.

Siegel, Benjamin R. "Markets of Pain: A Transnational History of the United States Opioid Crisis." Lecture, Colloquium on Global History, Freie Universität, Berlin, December 17, 2018.

Tagore, Rabindranath. "Gitanjali 35." The Poetry Foundation. Accessed April 27, 2023. Originally published 1913. https://www.poetryfoundation.org/poems/45668/gitanjali-35.

Troy, Mike, Jim Dudlicek, Bridget Goldschmidt, Gina Acosta, and Abby Klecker. *87th Annual Report.* Progressive Grocer, April 2020.

Turner, Jack. *Spice: The History of a Temptation.* New York: Vintage Books, 2004.

Food and Agriculture Organization of the United Nations, International Fund for Agriculture Development, UNICEF, World Food Programme, and World Health Organization. *The State of Food Insecurity and Nutrition in the World 2022: Repurposing Food and Agricultural Policies to Make Healthy Diets More Affordable.* Rome, Italy: Food and Agriculture Organization of the United Nations, 2022. https://doi.org/10.4060/cc0639en

United Nations Office on Drugs and Crime. *World Drug Report 2010.* New York: United Nations, 2010. https://www.unodc.org/unodc/en/data-and-analysis/WDR-2010.html.

Wallace-Wells, David. *The Uninhabitable Earth: Life After Warming.* New York: Tim Duggan Books, 2019.

READER NOTES

As this is a collection of creative nonfiction stories, some names, events, and details have been revised. Many characters, scenes, and experiences could not make it into the final story. As Virginia Woolf wrote, "Memory is the seamstress and a capricious one at that. Memory runs her needle in and out, up and down, hither and thither. We know not what comes next, or follows after. It's the perpetual dance of granite and rainbows in dealing with facts and story in memoir." This is just a slice of my story, but I did my best to weave the memories from grounded granite to bright rainbows.

Printed in the USA
CPSIA information can be obtained
at www.ICGtesting.com
LVHW101340190823
755600LV00008B/697

9 781544 544823